GP89 01799

*T*he *H*uman *S*ide of *P*roject *M*anagement

Ruth Sizemore House

Addison-Wesley Publishing Company Inc.

Reading, Massachusetts • Menlo Park, California • New York
Don Mills, Ontario • Wokingham, England • Amsterdam • Bonn
Sydney • Singapore • Tokyo • Madrid • San Juan

LIBRARY OF CONGRESS
Library of Congress Cataloging-in-Publication Data

House, Ruth.
    The human side of project management / Ruth Sizemore House.
        p.   cm.
    Include index.
    ISBN 0-201-12355-X
1. Industrial project management   2. Personnel management.
I. Title.
HD69.P75H68   1988
658.4′04—dc19   88-972
                                                             CIP

Cover design by Linda Koegel
Text design by Wendy Allen
Set in 10 point Bembo by Compset Inc., Beverly, Massachusetts

ISBN 0-201-12355-X
BCDEFGHIJ-AL-89
Second printing, October 1989

Contents

To Kenneth R. House:
My partner in work and in life.

*A*cknowledgments

Thank you, Martin Broadwell, for not waiting to say the right thing to the right person at the right time.

Thank you, Kenneth House, for not waiting to give encouragement and support.

Thank you, friends, for giving support (in part) *by* waiting:

- Scott Shershow who waited and waited on this manuscript.
- Mary Ashford, Ed Douglass, Margaret Douglass, Kenneth House, Katy Schwaderer and Janice Slocum who waited and waited on me while Scott waited on the manuscript.
- Westleigh Darrell House who, well, who actually waited on no one.

1

Dealing with Real Life

INTRODUCTION

"Life is what happens to you while you are making other plans."   A. J. Marshall

That old management maxim, "Plan your work and work your plan," is easier said than done. Neither life nor work waits while we make our plans. The clock keeps ticking. It's hard not to get frantic and lurch forward without a map. But in project management, traveling without a map is a guarantee we'll be racing across a treadmill. As one driven project manager put it, "I'm tired. And I'm tired of 'excellence.' I'd cheerfully settle for sane, controllable mediocrity if I could just get off this roller coaster."

Not only is it hard to find the *time* to make things better, it's also hard to find the *way* to make them better. It's easy enough, if you're willing to invest the time, to read this theory or that theory—to peruse busloads of research data.

Figure 1–1
The Aerodigm Corporation Organizational Chart

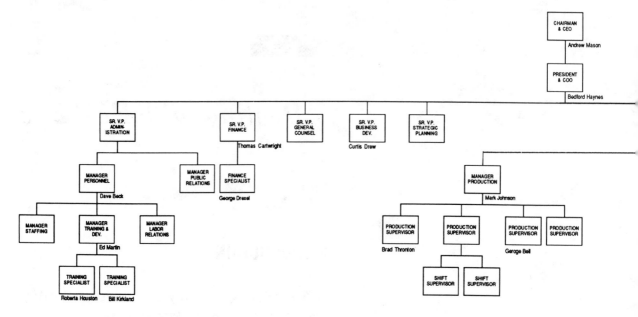

But putting those theories to work, applying the research to real life—that's the hard part. It's so difficult to make the translation that it often doesn't seem worth the time and trouble.

This book won't eliminate the need for effort on your part. It *can* make your exertion more efficient (1) by showing you how theory translates to practice in a fictitious company and (2) by transferring practice in the fictitious company to application in your real life. The setting for translating theory is the Aerodigm Corporation. The medium is a process which will be developed primarily through case studies. The vehicle for transferring the process back to your real life is the Project Partner, a final section in most chapters that you can use as a job aid. In this chapter we'll take a closer look at the setting for translating theory to practice, the medium for translating, and the vehicle for transfer.

THE SETTING

The Aerodigm Corporation is an aeronautical firm that includes both research and production. The core organization began as a family company, Airways Engineering. Since World War II, however, it has grown in leaps and bounds. It is now larger, more efficient, and—as the organization chart in Figure 1-1 shows—more complex than in the old days.

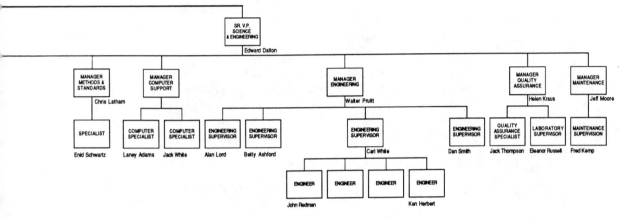

Crosscurrents among several of the top managers at Aerodigm influence the politics of projects:

Bedford Haynes, president and chief operating officer

Haynes is a graduate Mechanical Engineer and a Master of Business Administration. His family acquired a strong minority holding in Aerodigm before he came to Aerodigm as President two years ago. (The former president, Andrew Mason, is now chairman and CEO.) Haynes is very conservative financially. He's skittish about paper wheeling and dealing. He likes cash on the barrelhead transactions—not leveraged ones.

Thomas Cartwright, senior vice president, finance

Cartwright is often called "Colonel." His white hair, military bearing and booming, confident voice make a striking impression. Cartwright has the ability to sway people in his direction even when all previous decisions have gone the other way. He tends to present his ideas as rules or accepted facts. He's bright, thoroughly competent. He's clearly interested only in dollars. He's not concerned about the environment or about the company's public image.

Edward Dalton, senior vice-president, science and engineering

Dalton is a low-keyed but powerful rival of Thomas Cartwright. Like Cartwright, Dalton can be very persuasive. Unlike Cartwright, Dalton's loyalty is to the technology and to the mission not to the dollars. Dalton won't violate his principles, but you can expect him to oppose Cartwright whenever it's ethically possible.

And some middle managers will have even more direct impact:

Mark Johnson, production manager

Johnson is often in conflict with Walter Pruitt, the engineering manager. Among other things, Johnson has complained about the wording of engineering specifications, about sweatshop conditions in the plant, about company-wide standards. One way or another, Johnson implicates Pruitt in these complaints. But when it comes time for solutions . . . well, count Johnson out.

Chris Latham, methods and standards manager

Latham is a P.E. (professional engineer) with several advanced degrees. He's thoroughly competent as an engineer, but he's also thoroughly arrogant about his credentials. Whenever possible, he touts four-syllable words and long sentences. He generally gives the impression of being above it all.

Walter Pruitt, engineering manager

Pruitt really resents the time it takes to deal with interpersonal issues. Pruitt longs to simply avoid sources of conflict in the organization. He's great at the administrative end of management. But some people would call his style of supervision abandonment.

Jeff Moore, maintenance manager

Moore is often allied with Mark Johnson. He would also go a long way to undercut Walter Pruitt. Moore doesn't really like new team approaches. He'd rather tell and be told what to do. He generally feels that in-house projects are a waste of time.

Four project managers will be center stage:

Alan Lord, electronics engineer

Alan is managing a project which has only loosely defined outcomes. His assignment is to update plant control systems. Well, he's used to engineering much more complicated systems. He had expected smooth sailing. However, he now feels manipulated by his client, abandoned by his own management, and confounded by the behavior of his own team. Team members are Laney Adams, computer specialist; John Redmon, engineer; and George Bell, production supervisor.

Betty Ashford, engineer

Betty's project is another one with only loosely defined outcomes. Betty is working with Roberta Houston, a training specialist, and with George Drexel, a finance specialist. Each team member is experienced in his own specialty but uninitiated in the other two. Furthermore, this is the first major project assignment for each of the three.

Carl White, mechanical engineer

Carl's assignment is to work with one person from each branch of science and engineering to revise operations standards. Carl has had a hard time getting through a commitment to priorities so that work can be scheduled and staffing decisions (along with other administrative decisions) can be made. Carl's team members are Fred Kemp, maintenance supervisor; Brad Thornton, production supervisor; Enid Schwartz, methods and standards specialist; and Jack Thompson, quality assurance specialist.

Dan Smith, engineer

Dan is managing a large project with well-defined outcomes. But the company doesn't have experience in the project technology. It would be easy for Dan and his team members to concentrate so intently on the technical side of the project that they ignore each other. However, Dan's team will have fewer interpersonal complications than the others. We'll look in on his team from time to time, but we won't stay for an extended visit as we will with other teams.

THE MEDIUM

When project management research and human relations research combine, the result is a process that activates four keys to project success:

- Key I: Plan the Interaction.
- Key II: Take a Closer Look at How Personal Styles Will Affect Project Success.
- Key III: Handle the Conflict.
- Key IV: Provide for the Routine Care and Feeding of the Project Team.

As a preliminary, we'll take a look at the backdrop that project management research and human relations research provide (Chapters Two and Three).

Next, a case description will introduce each key. Then individual chapters will develop the step by step process that activates each key. As we go, we'll see how the project managers you've just met apply each step at Aerodigm. We'll see how they—

I. Plan the interaction needed to get results across the "knotted line" (Key I). ("Knotted line" describes many situations more accurately than "dotted line" does.)

   A. Identify the management tools that are likely to contribute most to project success (Chapters Four and Five).

   B. Visualize the key people and their locations across boundaries in the organization (Chapter Six).

   C. Analyze conflicting pressures in the organization and the impact an idea will have on them (Chapter Six).

   D. Build key elements into a negotiation plan (Chapter Six).

   E. Organize what they know about key people and the interaction among them to get an edge on personality conflict (Chapter Six).

   F. Build a win-win presentation into their negotiation styles (Chapter Six).

II. Take a closer look at how personal styles will affect project success (Key II).

   A. Explore their own personal styles (Chapter Seven).

   B. Realistically envision how personal styles will affect their project (Chapter Seven).

   C. Decide when to just "live and let live"; when to modify their own behavior; when to give and get feedback about the effect a relationship is having on the job; when to negotiate for changes in behavior (Chapter Seven).

III. Handle the conflict (Key III).

   A. Expect conflict and plan ahead how to handle it (Chapter Eight).

B. Have their own stress management techniques in place *before* the project begins (Chapter Eight).

C. Serve as a lightning rod: listen and reflect (Chapter Nine).

D. Excavate the real issues underlying a conflict (Chapter Nine).

E. Look for win-win alternatives (Chapter Ten).

F. Cut their losses when necessary (Chapter Ten).

IV. Provide for the routine "care and feeding" of their project teams (Key IV).

A. Identify the interpersonal roles and skills needed to maintain and complete group action (Chapter Eleven).

B. Encourage group performance of these roles and skills (Chapter Eleven).

C. Develop missing roles and skills in other team members when possible (Chapter Eleven).

D. Supply missing roles and skills when needed (Chapter Eleven).

E. Recognize dysfunctional roles (Chapter Twelve).

F. Balance dysfunctional roles (Chapter Twelve).

Finally, we'll review the process with a more detailed checklist that you can use as a job aid back in real life (Chapter Thirteen).

THE VEHICLE FOR TRANSFER

The Project Partner sections at the end of Chapters Four through Twelve can help you transfer the practices at Aerodigm back to real life. These sections contain worksheets and exercises you can apply to a current project back on the job. The entire Project Partner is repeated at the end of this book, on perforated pages which can be removed from this volume and photocopied for use with your future projects.

2

*M*anaging *P*rojects: *A S*pecial *C*ase

INTRODUCTION

VIETOR'S FUNNY BUSINESS

"We didn't exactly finish the project, but we did take a step toward the next step."

Copyright 1986, *USA TODAY*. Reprinted with permission.

It would be funnier if it weren't so true. Project management is different. Even an experienced line manager who has been assigned a project may feel he's facing an endless sequence of steps. And the steps even have steps.

As if that weren't enough, each step of a step has its own deadline and, as a result, its own pressure. One project manager put it succinctly: "We're in the business to make ulcers." And a number of textbook authors have agreed: "Projects have an inherent tendency to get out of control"; "projects tend toward entropy." The words are different; the sentiment is the same.

A few line managers might describe line management in the same doomsday terms. Most do not. Neither do textbook authors. Why is project management a special case?

Of course, the project technology could make ulcers. It could get out of control. It could tend toward entropy. But when people use those terms they are usually thinking of other project people not project technology.

Does a project result in personality change (as getting behind the steering wheel of a car sometimes does)? Does it create mass hysteria (as we used to see in monster movies such as *King Kong* and *Godzilla*)? Some would say, "Pretty close." But the real explanation lies in the complex relationships made necessary by the definition of "project" and by the purpose of a project approach. "Project" can be defined as an interrelated and primarily nonrepetitive set of activities which combine to meet certain objectives. The purpose of a project approach is to get maximum input from technical specialists and to do it efficiently. In this chapter we'll see how these inherent project conditions bring about relationships different from those in line management.

THE DEFINITION OF *PROJECT*

One more time. . . .

An interrelated and primarily non-repetitive set of activities which combine to meet certain objectives.

These tasks, for example, would qualify as projects:

- building a custom home;
- computerizing personnel records;
- engineering a rapid transit system.

These tasks would not qualify:

- building 116 identical apartment units;
- maintaining personnel records;
- manufacturing 54 transit vehicles.

Projects are different: each has a different combination of objectives; each has a different requirement for resources; each has a different environment. Some objectives may piggyback those in previous projects; but different combinations will require a new plan. Some reliable resources used in previous projects may be drawn on again; but different sequencing and a different marketplace will require new estimating, new evaluating, new scheduling. Some members of a previous project may work on the project team; but new priorities, new workload, new management will require a new analysis of the project environment and a new effort at team development.

Although he may work as if there's no tomorrow, the project manager needs to look at each project as if yesterday never happened. The nonrepetitive nature of a project results in task uncertainty. This isn't all bad. In fact, there's good reason to believe that project team members (especially in R & D) get along best and are happiest with their project manager when task uncertainty is high. But succeeding at an uncertain task will require close coordination with the parent organization and with the client. And high task uncertainty makes estimating time and materials tough. Some project managers would say useless. As a result they may ignore valuable planning and control techniques.

In one project, for example, the manager gave up pinning down objectives and controlling around them. His project was finally cancelled after its cost soared from $250,000 to $6.1 million and the time required mushroomed from nine months to over two years.

The nonrepetitive nature of a project also results in wide swings in resource needs. There will be times when team members feel they can't get enough done. Times when they can't get enough to do. Even when it has been carefully planned, a project will not need the same amount of time from the same kind of people throughout. There will be peaks and valleys. Both the work overload at the peaks and the boredom at the valleys can produce team dissatisfaction.

An industrial psychologist has this to say about the boredom. "When people become euphoric because it's Friday and depressed because it's Sunday night, that says a lot about how they feel about their work. How do you put a dollar value on that? There isn't enough money to compensate for a job that you hate" (Rice, 1985, p. 54).

And the interrelatedness of activities also has an affect on the peaks and valleys. Since many activities depend on the completion of a previous activity, one delay usually dictates many others. It has a domino effect. And if activities have been estimated accurately, playing catch-up is really difficult.

In a construction project, the domino effect might work like this. Control panels are late for delivery (the schedule suffers). Unsure when the panels will arrive, the subcontractor has people on standby (costs go up). When the panels finally arrive, the subcontractor puts people on overtime and works two shifts to make up for lost time (costs go up again). Under pressure from schedule and cost overruns, the subcontractor takes shortcuts in an attempt to catch up (technical quality suffers). Equipment fails to operate on a test run. It takes a day of troubleshooting to locate the problems: wiring errors resulting from time pressure and from shortcuts (the schedule suffers again). As a result, the work of a second subcontractor is delayed. (The impact—in sequence—on schedule, on cost, and on technical quality repeats itself.)

THE PURPOSE OF A PROJECT MANAGEMENT APPROACH

The project management approach is designed to get maximum input from technical specialists and to do it efficiently. In a line management operation, technical people often complain that their technical decisions are watered down by administrative decisions. The project management approach flattens the organization and makes that watering down less likely. For example, Betty Ashford (an engineer) manages a project that includes George Drexel (a financial specialist) and Roberta Houston (a training specialist). If Betty's project were to operate strictly within the limits of the organizational hierarchy, communicating with her project members would be cumbersome. George Drexel's technical input, for example, would be filtered through the senior vice-president of finance, the senior vice-president of science and engineering, and the manager of the engineering group. The odds of George's input reaching Betty intact are slim (see Figure 2-1).

But when the chain of command has committed money, time and staff, Betty's team can communicate using a project management model. Both George and Roberta can give their input directly to Betty. Betty can coordinate activities and keep the formal hierarchy informed (See Figure 2-2).

An entire organization built around project managers who borrow team members from functional managers is called a matrix

Figure 2–1
Communicating Within the Organizational Hierarchy

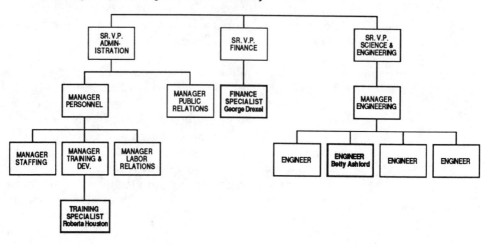

Figure 2–2
Communicating Using a Project Management Model

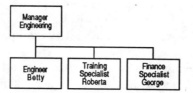

organization. This matrix organization changes previously informal lines of communication into formal, official ones (See Figure 2-3).

So in a project management operation, the technical input is more likely to remain intact. But traditional expectations about how things get done may get trampled. Position authority doesn't seem to have much impact. An entire project is likely to seem out of control, and a given person is likely to feel his own work is out of control as well. A project manager has responsibility without the authority to match. As if that weren't enough, she's likely to have a wider management span than her line management counterpart. It's no wonder that volatile situations are the order of the day.

The authority of position will not have the same control over people's behavior as it would in a strict line organization. Getting results will depend more on the influence of technical knowledge

Figure 2–3
Communicating Within a Matrix Model

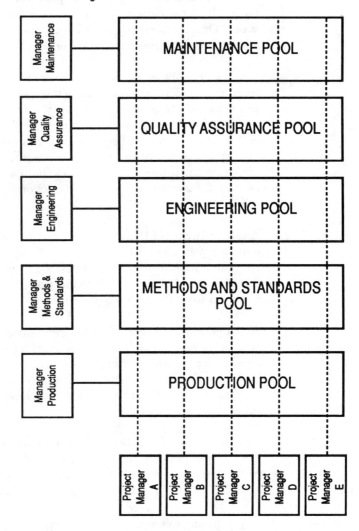

and ability. For example, Carl White (engineering) has representatives from four other departments on his project team. Carl doesn't control their salaries, their appraisals, their promotions. Their department managers control these things. Their department managers have the clout. Carl doesn't. If he wants cooperation, he'll need to earn the respect of team members through his technical ability and his skill in team management.

Because the nature of control is different, things are more likely to appear *out* of control. Even to the person in charge. Perhaps especially to the person in charge. One project manager put it this way: "The real advantage of project planning and control is that it's easier to see how much trouble you're in."

Carl could easily agree. To begin with his project spans five technologies. It must pull together five personalities (which often seem in conflict). And he must satisfy several levels of management with conflicting priorities. As if that weren't enough, his project will require several local permits; approvals from OSHA (Occupational Safety and Health Administration), EPA (Environmental Protection Agency), and the State Department of Natural Resources; and periodic checks on opportunities for minorities and women.

All the participants know Carl's project is both new and temporary. Because it is new, Carl will forge the chains of communication from scratch. Because it is temporary, he will exert extra effort to keep each link connected. (It would be easy for team members to be drawn away over time by other commitments.)

And a person can even feel that his individual contribution is out of control. A person may produce his work product for a peer in another department. Yet his division chief may control performance evaluation and salary review. There is not unity of command. Instead there is divided allegiance; there is a conflict in roles.

One member of Carl's team—Fred Kemp from maintenance—is caught right in the middle. His boss would do almost anything to undermine Carl's boss. Fred is afraid that any visible contribution he makes to this project will result in harassment by his boss.

Authority doesn't equal responsibility. A project manager is held responsible for getting the job done. But he may not have line authority over the people doing work for him.

Carl has a lot on his shoulders. And no line authority to help him out. But his job is on the line just the same. Regardless of the complications and the conflict, he will be held accountable for results.

Many management texts suggest a manager have no more than five to ten people reporting directly to him. But in a project organization, the span of management depends on the number of technologies or trades involved. If there are 30 technical areas and trades involved, a project manager may have 30 people reporting directly to him.

It's too soon to tell on this project. But Carl's last project required participation from a company financial specialist, a union representative, outside subcontractors, and his client in addition to his core of technical specialists. With all the conflict already on his hands, Carl's hoping the span of this project won't be as broad.

To make order out of chaos, project managers use project planning and control techniques like Gantt Charts, CPM (Critical Path Method), PERT (Project Evaluation and Review Technique), and GERT (Graphic Evaluation and Review Technique). Since a project is one-of-a-kind, no procedures or relationships can be taken for granted. Some graphic control technique is essential.

- The Gantt chart is among the earliest graphic aids to planning. It was developed around 1900 by Henry Gantt, a follower of Frederick Taylor. It is considered the Model T of project planning. But some project managers say it is superior to more elaborate techniques because of its simplicity.
- CPM visually identifies the sequence of activities that will have the longest duration. Any delay in this sequence will delay project completion. This technique was developed by DuPont to minimize downtime required for plant maintenance.
- PERT adds a statistical analysis to account for activity durations that cannot be accurately estimated. It was developed for the Polaris Submarine Project.
- GERT is applicable to research with a high predictable failure rate. A medical research project, for example, has significant chance of failing to meet its primary project objectives; but it has an excellent chance of contributing substantially to the objectives of some other project.

One consulting firm puts it to clients this way: "Project management and control techniques change the 'worry curve.' People tend to wait until the last 10 percent of a project to worry. Then it may be too late. With good project planning and control techniques, people worry from the very beginning. So they're more likely to spot problems in time to do something about them" (Clark, n.d., p. I-02).

Project mistakes are harder to hide. Suppose someone orders excess custom-made, precast concrete slabs, for example. The project manager can't simply save them for use the next time; there won't be any next time.

Efficiency comes through worrying right away. So may crankiness. As a result, volatile situations are likely to be the rule, not the exception. People working in a pressure cooker will have to let off steam. In Alan Lord's project, for example, one team member's boss interferes with team activity. Besides that, technical exchanges are often only thin disguises for a persistent personality clash. It's not surprising that Alan has a potential explosion on his hands.

SUMMARY

A project is an interrelated and primarily nonrepetitive set of activities which combine to meet certain objectives. Because activities are interrelated and nonrepetitive,

- task uncertainty is high, so planning and estimating can be especially frustrating;
- wide swings in resource needs may result in alternating overload and boredom;
- a delay in any one activity is likely to have the domino effect.

The project management approach is designed to get maximum input from technical specialists and to do it efficiently. Conditions built into the design mean that

- the authority of position has less influence than technical knowledge and ability;
- because the nature of control is different, things are more likely to appear to be *out* of control;
- there is not unity of command; there is divided allegiance;
- authority doesn't equal responsibility;
- if many technologies or trades are involved, the span of management will be wide;
- volatile situations are likely to be the rule, not the exception.

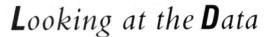

3

Looking at the Data

INTRODUCTION

"Except during the nine months before he draws his first breath, no man manages his affairs as well as a tree does." George Bernard Shaw

Well, no wonder. A tree isn't struggling with the same complex interpersonal relationships we project managers face (at least not as far as we know). If you're like many project managers, you've probably said to yourself more than once: "Not much I can do about it. That's just the way people are. After all, what do we really *know* about how people relate?"

We may not know things in human relationships with the same apparent certainty we do in mathematics or engineering. But we do have some substantial data. And the data suggest consistent patterns in the organization as a whole, in the project task, in the project team, and within the project manager. In this chapter we'll look at the data from which those patterns are derived.

THE DATA

To review the data, read through each of the following mini-cases. Select one of the multiple choice answers listed. Then read on to see if the research data surprise you.

Mini-case number one

One difference between project management and line management is the uncertainty of tasks. Sometimes outcomes can be only loosely defined or loosely agreed upon. And the extent of agreement over outcomes is one of the factors that decides which management tools will help a project manager the most. Another critical factor is the experience of the project team with the project technology. Together, these factors determine which tools the project manager will rely on the most: formal planning, formal control, team coordination (internal integration), or coordination outside the team (external integration).

It's easy for a project manager to assume that if he's using the Critical Path Method and having regular project control meetings, his progress will be smooth. But formal planning and formal control are only two of the standard project management tools available. Two that are often ignored are team coordination and coordination outside the team (with the client and with management in the parent organization).

Four project managers are commiserating about their trials and tribulations. Which one do you think is best in touch with the special requirements of his or her project?

A. Alan is managing a project which has only loosely defined outcomes. But he considers it a lucky break that the company has a lot of experience in the project technology. He figures that if he uses good planning techniques like the Critical Path Method and strong formal controls, he'll have few difficulties.

B. Betty's project is another one with only loosely defined outcomes. Unfortunately, the company isn't experienced in the project technology. She expects formal planning and controls will be a snap compared to the squabbling that will go on within the team over whose way is the right way.

C. Carl's project has well-defined outcomes. In addition, the company is quite experienced in the project technology. Like Betty, Carl expects his biggest problem will be developing teamwork within his group.

D. Dan is managing a large project with well-defined outcomes. But the company doesn't have experience in the project technology. He plans to concentrate on close coordination with his clients.

The research suggests Carl (Choice C) is right on target. In a project with well-defined outcomes and high team experience with the project technology, skills in the internal team coordination are likely to be relied on more than skills in coordination outside the team, formal planning, or formal control (McFarlan, 1981, p. 149).

As for the other choices, Alan (Choice A) may be in for some tough going. In a project with loosely defined outcomes and high team experience with the technology, formal planning and formal controls are likely to contribute the least of the management tools Alan has available. He'd do better to concentrate on coordination outside the team (with his client and with top management in his parent organization) and within his team (McFarlan, 1981, p. 149).

Betty's concern (Choice B) about squabbling within her team may not be as big a problem as she expects. In a project with loosely-defined outcomes and low team experience with the technology, getting her team to pull together is likely to demand less of her than coordination outside her team, formal planning techniques, or formal control techniques (McFarlan, 1981, p. 149).

Communication outside the team has increased importance if the team is working on a research project. But external communication is often ignored. In fact, it's often scorned—it smacks of office politics. Team members—including the project manager—may feel that being good at their jobs should be enough. To better coordinate communication outside the project team, a project manager can

- select clients as project team members;
- place clients in key positions on the team;
- involve clients in key decisions like approval of specifications and of key action dates;
- clearly define areas of client responsibility (such as the management of a change control process, education about a new system, installation of the system);
- communicate formally with other members of the client group (encourage frequent, in-depth meetings of a client steering committee; distribute frequent, detailed project team minutes to key members of the client group);

- communicate systematically with key people in the organization as a whole (such as progress reports to a corporate steering committee) (McFarlan, 1981, p. 149).

Dan's interpersonal efforts (Choice D) may pay off, but he should expect the greatest return from his efforts in formal planning and formal control techniques. In a large project with well-defined outcomes and low team experience with the task, they are his most valuable tools.

Mini-case number two

Swings in the need for resources can mean alternating overload and boredom for a given individual. Boredom and the in-fighting that usually go with it mean that team coordination is especially important.

In Carl's project (with well-defined outcomes, high team experience with the technology), team coordination tools are likely to be critical. These tools include the following (McFarlan, 1981, p. 149):

- selection of experienced technical people to project team;
- selection of team members who have worked together before;
- selection of project manager (of course, in this case, Carl is already it);
- communication within the team (frequent team meetings, regular distribution to team members of key design decisions, regular technical status reviews);
- involvement of team members in setting goals and deadlines;
- low turnover (Turnover on project teams has been tied directly to productivity. Among R & D teams, for example, groups between 1.5 and 5.0 years are significantly more productive than others. [Birnbaum and others, 1979, pp. 657–658]. Controlling turnover in line management is important; in project management it is critical. And since turnover typically goes up with dissatisfaction on the job, the importance of the human element again comes to the forefront);
- outside technical assistance (When the project team is disagreeable, an outside person can mediate. When the project team is on the verge of a bad decision through

being too agreeable, an outside person can be the devil's advocate).

One of these tools, communication within the team has the greatest relative importance if the project belongs in which one of these categories?

> A. a technical service project (project with a mature technology that involves maintaining or improving an established product or service);
> B. a development project (a project with a less developed technology);
> C. a research project (a project with an essentially undeveloped technology).

The research suggests that in technical service projects (Choice A), which typically deal with relatively mature technologies, communication across organizational boundaries doesn't seem to be as critical (Katz, 1982, p. 82). In a development project (Choice B), communication across organizational boundaries seems to be just as important as communication within the team. High performance in a research project (Choice C) doesn't seem to be as closely related to communication within the team. Surprisingly, it's related to a high level of communication with professionals outside the organization.

Mini-case number three

Because project activities are interrelated, one problem is likely to generate another—to have a domino effect. So the ability to contain the cost of the initial problem affects a project manager's performance. Which of these statements characterizes high-performing project managers?

> A. They managed low-turnover groups
> B. They believed that many things were beyond their control
> C. They encouraged open discussion of disagreement
> D. A. and C. above
> E. All of the above

The research suggests all of the above (Choice E). High performing project managers

> • managed low-turnover groups (Birnbaum and others, 1979, pp. 657–658);

- believed many things were beyond their control (Dailey, 1981, p. 46). Some traits officially encouraged by an organization may be dysfunctional in a project management setting. For example, a strong sense of control over situations is usually encouraged (and sought after) in line managers. But in one study, high-performing project managers reported that they believed a number of things were outside their control: they registered an external locus of control on the Rotter Internal-External Orientation Survey (Dailey, 1981, p. 46).
- encouraged open discussion of disagreement (Birnbaum and others, 1979, pp. 657–658; Hill, 1977, p. 52). In some line operations, managers are considered strong if they stifle conflict—keep their people in line. A project manager who stifles conflict is likely to be building a time bomb. A project manager can help by pacing the passage through a conflict so it doesn't get out of hand. But the passage must often be through—not around—the problem. And open discussion of problems seems to be the surest route. The project manager most likely to steer safe passage is the project manager who acts as a lightning rod, serves as a role model, sees some usefulness in conflict, sets an example of listening and counsels (Birnbaum and others, 1979, pp. 657–658; Hill, 1977, pp. 52–56).

Mini-case number four

A project manager's line authority may not help him get results as much as his ability to influence others. He may often be crossing organizational boundaries to get input and cooperation. He will depend on people he has no line authority over (like specialists in other divisions or contractors) to get work done. A person's closeness to organizational boundaries (researchers call this boundary relevance) is the strongest single predictor of role conflict. The conflict is heightened if the boundary separates an organization and the outside world (Miles, 1976, p. 177). Role conflict is one of the conditions that makes projects seem out of control. And it is a significant factor because it correlates with all but one of these undesirables. Which one?

    A. Homicide rate
    B. Distortion and suppression of information
    C. Violation of chain of command
    D. Tendency to leave the organization

The research suggests that oddly enough there's actually a negative correlation between role conflict and homicide rate (Choice A) (Lester, 1973, p. 774). But role conflict correlates positively with distortion and suppression of information (Think what those can do to a project team!); violation of chain of command; and tendency to leave the organization. It also correlates positively with

- goal conflict and inconsistency;
- delay in decision;
- frustration;
- tension;
- sense of threat and anxiety;
- psychological withdrawal;
- sense of futility;
- acting out, projection, contrived interpersonal conflict, hostility (House, 1982, p. 15).

Mini-case number five

Which of these classic management principles is likely to be the most useful to Alan, Betty, Carl and Dan?

    A. Authority equals responsibility
    B. Unity of command—each employee must report to only one supervisor
    C. Efficiency through specialization
    D. None of the above

The research suggests that none of the classic management principles (Choice D) really contributes much to the project management situation. In fact, effective project managers must make drastic departures from classic management techniques (Greiner and Schoin, 1981, p. 17). As for the other choices, authority might equal responsibility (Choice A) in other parts of the organization. But project managers have responsibility for the success of a project without having the usual line authority over many of the people who contribute to it. Project members typically see their functional supervisors as having the clout (in the form of appraisals and incentives, for example). So the project manager's effectiveness is likely to depend more on his ability to influence than on the authority of his position.

In other parts of the organization, each person may report to only one supervisor (Choice B). But on a project team, specialists will have divided allegiance—to the project manager, to their functional supervisors, and to the leaders of other projects on which they work. Not only does this multiple supervision pose tricky problems for the project manager, it may bewilder the specialists themselves. People are likely to be confused about who's responsible for what decision and who talks to whom about what.

The rest of the organization may gain efficiency through specialization (Choice C), but efficiency on a project team depends on getting the $2 + 2 = 5$ effect by combining the specialties represented. So a project manager must generate cooperation that spans the loyalties of particular technologies and particular organizational segments.

Mini-case number six

Volatile situations are likely to be the rule, not the exceptions. Top among the volatile issues will be: project priorities, administrative procedures, technical opinions and performance trade-offs, manpower resources, cost estimates, personality conflicts, and the scheduling and sequencing of work. For all issues but one, the intensity of conflict will likely vary depending on the stage of the project (Hill, 1977, 45). Which issue will remain a relatively constant source of conflict throughout project formation, buildup, maintenance, and phase-out?

    A. Administrative procedures
    B. Technical opinions and performance trade-offs
    C. Personality conflicts
    D. Scheduling and sequencing of work

The research suggests that personality conflict (Choice C) is most likely to persist throughout the life of a project. In fact,

"Project managers emphasized that personality conflicts are particularly difficult to handle. Even apparently small and infrequent personality conflicts might be more disruptive and detrimental to overall program effectiveness than intense conflict over nonpersonal issues which can often be handled on a more rational basis" (Hill, 1977, p. 46).

Mini-case number seven

High performing project managers are more likely than low performing managers to deal with interpersonal conflict in which of these ways?

A. Personal absorption of aggression
B. Role modeling
C. Sense of some usefulness in a conflict
D. Pacing and control of potential conflict
E. B. and C. above
F. A. and D. above
G. All of the above

The research suggests that high performing project managers are more likely than low-performing ones to deal with conflict in all of these ways (Choice G). In addition they are more likely to encourage openness and emotional expression, set an example of listening, and counsel (Hill, 1977, pp. 552–556).

By now you may be feeling a lot of conflict over your role as project manager. The research data backs up practical experience: there are substantial differences between line management and project management. How can you react to them? We'll look at some specific suggestions in the next part of this chapter.

Both the real-life experiences of project managers and the research data point to the importance of interpersonal relationships to project success. Both suggest that a systematic approach to interpersonal relationships can be as important to project success as a systematic approach to project planning and control.

But is it possible to approach relationships systematically? Possible without being manipulative or tyrannical? Yes, it is possible. Using one systematic approach, a project manager could

- plan the interaction needed to get results across the knotted line;
- take a closer look at how project success can be affected by his expectations about control and his preferences in relationship styles;
- expect conflict and plan ahead how to deal with it;
- provide for the routine care and feeding of his project team.

Throughout the rest of the book we'll develop the steps that activate each of these keys.

SUMMARY

Research data backs up what experienced project managers say about the differences between line management and project management.

- There is greater task uncertainty. And task uncertainty is one of the primary factors to consider when selecting the project management tools likely to benefit a project the most.
- Wide swings in the need for resources can result in alternating boredom and overload.
- Project activities are interrelated. So a problem in one is likely to have a domino effect on later activities.
- Authority of position may have less effect on project success than the ability to influence people in other ways. Things may seem out of control. The resulting role conflict can cause serious problems.
- Classic management principles (like unity of command, authority equals responsibility, a limited span of control) simply may not hold up.
- Volatile situations are the rule, not the exception.

A systematic approach to managing interpersonal relationships can help. The project manager can:

- plan the interaction needed to get results across the knotted line;
- take a closer look at how his personal style will affect project success;
- expect conflict and plan ahead how to deal with it;
- provide for the routine care and feeding of his project team.

✦ Key I ✦

PLAN THE INTERACTION NEEDED TO GET RESULTS ACROSS THE KNOTTED LINE

The Case of Alan Lord

Alan Lord is an electronics engineer. He's managing a project with only loosely defined outcomes. Originally he considered it a lucky break that his team has a lot of experience with the project technology. He figured that if he used good planning techniques like the Critical Path Method and strong formal controls, he would have few difficulties.

Alan's assignment is to update plant control systems. Well, he's used to engineering much more complicated systems. So he expected smooth sailing. But now he feels—

—manipulated by his client, the production manager, Mark Johnson. The vice-president of science and engineering authorized the project because Johnson claimed his people were working under sweatshop conditions. But now that Alan has undertaken the project, Johnson's definition of the problem keeps changing and he seems reluctant to give Alan access to key members of the production staff. Alan wonders if Johnson manufactured the complaint originally just to put Alan's boss, the engineering manager, under fire. Johnson seems to blame engineering for all his problems: for excessive overtime ("Poorly engineered specs," he says.); for equipment downtime; for personnel turnover.

—abandoned by his management. Walter Pruitt, engineering manager and Alan's boss, has such a low opinion of Johnson that he can hardly stand to hear the man's name. Pruitt's last words to Alan about the project were, "Leave me out of it. Just get the So-and-So off our backs."

—confounded by the behavior of his own team. One team member believes no automated control system will do the job under plant conditions. Another (the computer specialist) thinks the project is a profound bore. And the third member (from production) is frequently absent from team meetings and seems unwilling to contribute when he is there.

In the following chapters, we'll see how Alan can plan the interaction among the people whose cooperation he needs. Next go round, he'll use this key before the project gets underway. But there's still time on this one to

- identify the management tools that are likely to contribute most to project success (Chapters Four and Five);
- visualize the boundaries in the organization and the location of key people across those boundaries (Chapter Six);
- analyze conflicting pressures in the organization and the impact the project will have on them (Chapter Six);
- build key elements into a negotiation plan (Chapter Six);
- organize information about key people and the interaction between them to get an edge on personality conflict (Chapter Six);
- build a win-win presentation into negotiation style (Chapter Six).

4

Choosing the Right Management Tools

INTRODUCTION

First, one philosophical question—what do an ice skater and a project manager have in common? Well, they are both subject to Kepler's Third Law of the Conservation of Angular Momentum (more or less):

As the circular path of an object becomes smaller and smaller, the object's speed gets faster and faster.

The House Project Management Corollary goes like this:

A project manager who tries to defy Kepler's Third Law of the Conservation of Angular Momentum by pulling controls closer and closer to his chest will travel faster and faster in smaller and smaller circles.

Skeptical? So was Frank Jarman, the MIT engineer who took over the apparel industry giant Genesco in 1973. Jarman's predecessor had emphasized sales alone; Jarman assigned himself the major project of reorienting the company toward profit. Jarman was a "bean counter." He imposed numerous, strict, quantitative controls and discounted the input of his managers. And instead of tapping the input from fashion-conscious, trend-setting old-timers, Jarman cut them out:

"Artistry's essential at the right level, but when you have a businessman running an operation and designers feeding into it, then it's unmaintainable. . . . Engineering companies are easier to understand, and you can apply scientific measurement to them so much more rapidly" (Carruth, 1975).

He proceeded to add more and more layers of management between him and the fashion specialists and to require more and more hard data. When the numbers didn't endorse his management style he literally presented each of his top managers with a hangman's noose.

As CEO, Jarman, of course, had some line authority. Plenty, you say? Well, it wasn't enough to compensate for ignoring the knotted lines. In January 1977, the Genesco board of directors ousted him (Carruth and others, 1977).

Jarman appears to have ignored all but one of the management tools available to project managers: formal controls. Others available to him were formal planning, internal integration, and external integration. In the rest of this chapter we'll see

- how to select those tools likely to contribute most to project success;
- how to use the tool of internal integration.

In the next chapter we'll see

- how to use the tool of external integration.

HOW TO SELECT THOSE TOOLS LIKELY TO CONTRIBUTE MOST TO PROJECT SUCCESS

A project organization has an inherent tendency to get out of control. So managers are tempted to apply double doses of classical management techniques in response. Then Kepler's Third Law comes into play. The more they pull back decision-making authority, the more they overinvolve themselves in work they've already delegated, the more intensely they focus on developing procedures of greater and greater detail—the more likely their project teams will be overloaded or straitjacketed into ineffectiveness.

Classical management techniques just won't hold up in the project management setting. Frank Moolin, Jr., who managed the Alaskan Pipeline Project, described the inadequacy of classical management this way:

"The informal organization structure and communication network is what makes organizations tick. As soon as managers learn to put aside petty territorial prerogatives they should nurture, cultivate, and encourage the informal organization structure to function. . . . It almost sounds contradictory that I should say that control is enhanced by encouraging the informal organization to work. Yet, that is exactly the case. That is particularly true when one also realizes that professionals of many different callings are essential to giant projects. I have found that the best method of insuring the necessary communication in giant projects is to bring together many participants of a flat organizational structure, set the example, encourage dialogue. . ." (Moolin, 1978, p. 8).

Specifically, expect these startling departures from classical management principles.

- Authority won't equal responsibility. Your success will depend more on your influence than on your authority.
- Most employees won't be reporting to only one supervisor. They'll have divided allegiance: to you, to their functional supervisor, to other project managers.
- Efficiency won't come through specializing but through combining specialties.

But activating the informal network doesn't mean abandoning all formal planning and control—it doesn't mean cultivating chaos. It's all a question of balance. How can you be sure you correctly select and balance your choice of project management tools? Let's take a closer look at Alan Lord's project to see.

Alan Lord is an electronics engineer. He's managing a project with only loosely defined outcomes. Originally he considered it a lucky break that his team has a lot of experience with the project

Table 4–1
Management Tools that Contribute to Project Success

Experience with Technology	Outcomes	
	Loosely-defined Outcomes	Well-defined Outcomes
High Company Experience	Internal Integration External Integration	Internal Integration
Low Company Experience	External Integration Formal Control Formal Planning (if project is large)	Formal Control Formal Planning (if project is large)

Based on McFarlan, T. Warren. "Portfolio Approach to Information Systems," Harvard Business Review, 59 *(5), Sept./Oct. 1981, 142–150.*

technology. He figured that if he used good planning techniques like the Critical Path Method and strong formal controls, he would have few difficulties. Alan's assignment is to update plant control systems. Well, he's used to engineering much more complicated systems. So he expected smooth sailing.

We can process Alan's project through Table 4-1 to see if his expectations were realistic.

Alan's project team is experienced in the project technology. With a good, experienced team and a good PERT Chart or Critical Path it does seem like the project should be a snap. But because of his team's experience they are likely to rely less on formal planning. Some team members may even feel it isn't needed at all. (It still is.) And they are likely to be impatient with the usual control procedures. ("We know what we're doing . . . that stuff is just a waste of time!") And the contrariness will be even worse if the team members feel the task has no challenge.

Alan expected cooperation and congeniality from his experienced team. But what has actually happened? Alan is confounded by the behavior of his own team. One team member believes no automated control system will do the job under plant conditions. Another (the computer specialist) thinks the project is a profound bore. And the third member (from production) is frequently absent from team meetings and seems unwilling to contribute when he is there.

Because Alan's team has high experience in the project technology, internal integration (developing cooperation within the team) will be one of his most important tools.

What if Alan had a less experienced project team? Well, the odds are that the challenge of the task would attract the attention of team members, allowing less time for bickering. Internal integration would probably be less difficult. And formal control systems would assume greater importance. With a large project, formal planning would also deserve more emphasis.

Alan didn't even consider the impact of loosely defined goals. He wasn't prepared for the confusion that can result when priorities or even objectives shift after a project is underway. And it didn't occur to him that these shifts would affect the kind of support he got from his own management. Alan thought an experienced team could carry the project without outside support.

What has actually happened? Alan now feels manipulated by his client, the production manager, Mark Johnson. Higher management authorized the project because Johnson claimed his people were working under sweatshop conditions. But now that Alan has undertaken the project, Johnson's definition of the problem keeps changing and he seems reluctant to give Alan access to key members of the production staff. Alan wonders if Johnson manufactured the complaint originally just to put Alan's boss, the engineering manager under fire. Johnson seems to blame engineering for all his problems: for excessive overtime ("Poorly engineered specs," he says.); for equipment downtime; for personnel turnover.

And Alan feels abandoned by his management. Walter Pruitt, Engineering Manager and Alan's boss, has such a low opinion of Johnson that he can hardly stand to hear the man's name. Pruitt's last words to Alan about the project were, "Leave me out of it. Just get the So-and-So off our backs."

Because Alan's project has loosely defined outcomes, external integration (developing cooperation outside the project team) will be one of his most important tools.

What if the project had static, well-defined outcomes? Then Alan's project would probably see much smoother sailing. The tools most critical to his success would be determined by his project team's level of experience.

The relative importance of external integration and internal integration can also be affected by the nature of the project task (Katz, 1982, p. 82).

- In a research project (development of new knowledge or concepts), helpful information is likely to be drawn from professionals outside the project team—probably outside the company as well. So external integration takes on added importance.
- In a technical service project (improvement of existing systems based on existing knowledge), the critical information is likely to lie within the project team. So internal integration takes on added importance.
- In a development project (combination of new knowledge applied to existing concepts), both external integration and internal integration are likely to be of equal importance.

For more information about formal planning and formal control, you can consult references on the technical side of project management. For more information about internal integration and external integration, read on.

HOW TO USE THE TOOL OF EXTERNAL INTEGRATION

Frank Moolin seems pessimistic about the prospect of smooth external integration:

"I don't have to tell you that owners are not satisfied with the results of their giant projects. They are not satisfied with the performance of their own engineers, with engineering organizations, with contractors and with constructors. You can often sense a corporate management level shrug of the shoulders . . . 'What else can we do?'" (Moolin, 1978, p. 3)

And Moolin has good reason to be pessimistic. External integration is one of the most difficult tools to use well. In the first place, it smacks of office politics. And most of us would rather think being good at our jobs is enough to ensure success. In the second place, "external" covers a lot of territory. It's easy to name the specific individuals on the project team; it's a lot more difficult to pinpoint those people outside the team who, for one reason or another, have an important stake. In the third place, we're likely to encounter conflicts among those outsiders with a stake in the project. And taking on more conflict seems like borrowing trouble.

But the cost of ignoring external integration is too high, as the following examples illustrate.

New York Telephone's recovery (with the help of other Bell System Companies) from an extraordinary service crisis in 1969 was itself extraordinary. But the cost of the crisis was well over $110 million. And the cause? Analysts generally agree the primary cause was the poor quality of communication between the thinkers at Bell Labs and the doers in the operating companies throughout the design of Electronic Switching Stations (Brooks, 1975, pp. 294–295).

The cost to Jay Forrester was more personal. His Project Whirlwind achieved staggering technical success. It advanced the state of computer technology ten years, developed the core of the SAGE air defense system, and generated entire organizations like Lincoln Labs, the MITRE Corporation, and Digital Computer Corporation. But in Forrester's pursuit of technological excellence, he overshot the goals and the restrictions of his original sponsors (the Office of Naval Research and MIT). When MIT organized Lincoln Laboratories as a direct result of Project Whirlwind, Forrester was excluded (Redmond & Smith, 1977, pp. 50–59).

And the cost to a client can be staggering. In the late 1950s, one aerospace firm decided to make up for lost time by proceeding with phase-three development before phase-two test results were complete. Phase-two results uncovered a major design flaw just before the phase-three missile was to blast off from Cape Canaveral. Rather than admit the problem and delay the test flight (and, presumably, their cash) the aerospace firm said nothing. The phase-three missile lurched up, over, and into the ocean (taking millions of tax dollars with it) (Gibson, 1981, p. 50).

External integration is difficult but too costly to ignore. What steps can a project manager take to effectively use this important tool?

1. Select clients as project team members.
2. Place clients in key positions on project teams.
3. Involve clients in key decisions such as approval of specifications and of key action dates.
4. Clearly define areas of client responsibility (such as management of a change control process, education about a new system, installation of the system).

5. Communicate formally with other members of the client group.
6. Communicate systematically with key people in your organization as a whole—as with progress reports to a corporate steering committee.

Let's take another look at Alan's project to see how it stacks up so far and what he has left to do.

Select clients as project team members

Well, there is a member of the client group on Alan's project team—George Bell. But in this case, Alan didn't make the selection. George was assigned to the project by his manager, Mark Johnson (who is, unfortunately, an enthusiastic adversary of Alan's manager).

If Alan had been given a choice, he would have probably made another selection. George is technically competent—an essential criteria. But, in the first place, Alan would have chosen an opinion leader from the client group. An opinion leader is someone who has a strong positive influence over the official decision maker. In the second place, he would have chosen someone with whom he had worked well before. If no one fit that bill, he would have looked for someone who at least had a good track record on interdepartmental projects.

How does George compare to the ideal client team member? His strength is his technical competence. But he's only been at Aerodigm a short time—not long enough to become an opinion leader with Mark Johnson. Besides, he and Johnson aren't likely candidates for a close working relationship. He doesn't like Johnson's abrupt, authoritarian style, even though he's grown accustomed to that style elsewhere. He's never worked with Alan before. Although he finds Alan's more relaxed, more democratic style appealing, he's rather bewildered by it. This will be his first interdepartmental project, and he can't decide which way to go. Should he emulate the tough-guy image of his own manager or follow the more easygoing lead of Alan's? Will team members from other departments see him as a boor or as a wimp?

George satisfies the two minimum requirements here—he is a member of the client group and he is competent. But he isn't an opinion leader in his own department and he is not experienced in working with interdepartmental teams. So Alan will need to

- develop George as an interdepartmental team member. He can see to it that George has a meaningful position on the team. He can be sure that George takes part in key decisions.
- nurture George's influence in the client department. He can help clarify what responsibilities the client department must assume in order for the project to succeed. And he can help George develop a strategy for winning the necessary support.
- keep the bases covered. He can communicate formally and regularly through George to other members of the client group. And—because of the adversarial stance of George's supervisor—he will take extra care to be sure management in the organization as a whole stays up to date on the project.

Place clients in key positions on project teams

Alan will have to work at this one, too. It's not that George seems uncooperative—he's just inexperienced and unsure of what's expected of him. Alan can't afford for George to be a team member in name only. So Alan will need to manage the team in a way that ensures George's participation.

Alan can assign a specific role to each team member for a project meeting. And he can rotate those roles from one meeting to the next.

- One team member can be the official historian. He can review the agenda at the beginning of a meeting and then help keep the group on track by periodically summarizing "What We've Done" and "What We Have Left to Do." At the end of the meeting, he can turn in his written summary to Alan who will have it typed and distributed to all team members.
- One team member can be the official conscience for the meeting to be sure that no alternatives or potential problems go unnoticed.
- One team member can be the official gatekeeper. He will see to it that every team member has the opportunity to speak on each issue. He can be sure no one is crowded out of the conversation by saying something such as "Wait a minute, we haven't heard from Laney yet." Or he can draw out a quiet team member by saying something such as "John, how do you feel about this?"

- One member can be the official time keeper. He can post the group on "Elapsed Time" and "Time Left to Go" to help keep the group from getting bogged down on a particular issue without realizing. Official time keeper is *not* the same role as nag. It's important that the time keeper not use his role to impose his own priorities on the group: he should not be more permissive when the topic is of special interest to him and then rush the group through other topics. He should simply regularly let the group know the status of time, "We're 15 minutes into our meeting now. We have 45 minutes left."

Alan can see to it that George fills one of these roles at each meeting (not always the same one). And he can let George know ahead of time what will be expected of him.

When the project team reports to top management, to the client, to other outside groups, Alan will be sure that George has an equal opportunity to represent the team publicly.

Involve clients in key decisions like approval of specifications and key action dates

All project team members, including the client member, should be notified of key decisions and key action items at least twice. Once before the project meeting when the agenda is distributed. Once after the meeting when the summary is distributed.

Several days before each meeting, an agenda should be distributed to team members. The agenda should remind team members to prepare some standard information. And it should identify key decisions and key action items that the project manager expects to surface. A sample from Alan's project appears in Figure 4–1.

Key action items and key decisions should appear a second time in a meeting summary. In fact, some project managers insist that a table of these items come first in a meeting summary. A sample from one of Alan's project meetings appears in Figure 4–2.

Figure 4–1
Sample Project Meeting Agenda Reminder

Date: August 15, 19XX
From: Alan Lord *Alan Lord*
To: George Bell
Subject: Plant Control Systems Project Meeting
            August 18

Please bring the standard project information to our
August 18 meeting in a form that is easy to retrieve
and simple to report.

* Your updated schedule.
* The time estimated to complete your portion
  of the project.
* The cost of your portion of the project to
  date.
* A listing of current problems and
  alternative solutions under consideration
  (with the pros and cons of each alternative
  identified).
* A listing of anticipated problems and
  possible alternative solutions (with the
  pros and cons of each alternative
  identified).

In addition, be prepared to discuss these decisions:

* How can we most economically compensate for
  the delay in delivery of the H-1 circuit
  panels?
* How can we enforce change controls at the
  lowest possible level?

And be prepared to commit dates on these action items

* Submit man hour estimates for your
  division's involvement in project.
* Submit estimate of staff support needed.

P.S. George, I expect the discussion about change controls to get hot & heavy. So please act as our gatekeeper during the meeting to be sure everyone gets a chance to comment on the subject.

        A.L.

Figure 4–2
Sample Summary of Key Decisions and Key Action Items

Please review these action items and these decisions with key people in your own division and either confirm your concurrence or report any reservations to me by the close of business on August 20, 19XX.

Action Item	Responsible Team Member	Action Date	Support Required
1. Design circuit panel to replace H-1.	John	September 5	Automation input from Laney by August 25.
2. Get sign off on change control system by immediate managers & report any problems to Alan right away.	Alan, George, Laney	August 20	Alan will follow up on problems identified.
3. Cancel order for H-1 circuit panels.	George	Immediately	None

Decision	Team Members Affected		Effective Date
We will handle change requests by using attached change control procedure.	Everyone		Immediately. (Alan will troubleshoot. See Action Item 2 above.)

This same table, left blank, is an excellent way for the historian to organize his meeting notes as well. It eliminates the need to record a number of "He said's" and "She said's" and helps focus attention on what should be remembered for later discussion or action.

Clearly define areas of client responsibility

This can easily be one of the toughest jobs for a project manager. Many clients expect to simply purchase a project without accepting any responsibility for making it work. In the case of Alan's project, it seems that Mark Johnson may even actively do some things that prevent the project from working. Alan can't afford to take anything for granted (not even that Mark would return Alan's phone calls, for example). So Alan should see to it that client responsibilities are clearly defined in writing from the beginning and that they are updated in writing whenever a change in objectives or a change in procedure makes it necessary to do so. A draft of client responsibilities should be ready by the second time a project manager discusses a project. In its revised form, it should be part of the project agreement. And updated versions should be given to the client as they are made. One format for tracking client responsibilities looks like Table 4-2.

Table 4–2
Table of Client Responsibilities
Objective _____

Activity	Duration	Client Time Required	Other Client Support/Conditions	Cost

Alan's complete table should include the responsibilities of the Production Division to (1) to help establish clear objectives and parameters early in the project; (2) to respond to project inquiries and to notify project team on certain critical issues within a specified turn-around time; (3) to manage a change control process; (4) to educate client employees about the project, their involvement, and the use of the outcome; (5) to operate and maintain the new system.

The change control process deserves special emphasis. Alan should have established from the very beginning that whenever a project objective changes after the initial agreement, the cost to the client will change also.

Communicate formally with other members of the client group

This will be especially awkward in Alan's project because of Mark Johnson's hostility and because of George Bell's inexperience. So Alan is working through George and in his presence to inform the client group and to build support within the client group.

With George, Alan asked Mark Johnson for the names of key users of the new systems and for the official okay to communicate directly with them. In addition, Alan has encouraged George to keep in regular contact with managers of every person affected in the Client Responsibility Table.

Communicate systematically with key people in the organization as a whole—as with progress reports to a corporate steering committee

Sometimes Alan has been tempted to just avoid the rest of the organization—and avoid the hassle. After all, Walter Pruitt has said "Leave me out of it." And surely, as the saying goes, "It's easier to get forgiveness than permission." But isolation has its risks, too. If

Alan loses touch with the company's mainstream, he runs the risk of making a huge investment in perfecting something of no value to the organization. And if he lets management stay at arm's length, they are likely to notice only the cost of his project, not the value of it.

Alan's team could strive for technical perfection in tasks that may not be worth doing at all. Frank Moolin commented on this dilemma:

"I like to describe my early engineering education as a 'rivet pitch' education . . . I learned everything there was about the number and spacing of rivets in the end of a truss member of a bridge, but I did not learn whether or not to build the bridge" (Moolin, 1978, p. 2).

Only by interacting with the rest of the organization can Alan know if the bridge (or the control system) is worth building.

And another risk of isolation is that management will see only cost, not value. There's an inherent tendency in many organizations for management to overvalue its career management staff and devalue its career technical staff. One research team uncovered many incidents like this one:

"Recently one of our scientists, who had a position near the top of the technical ladder, had a frustrating experience. He requested a table for his work area and was given a wooden one. A few weeks later the facilities manager replaced it with a metal table, explaining that only managers were issued wooden ones. The scientist became so upset that he left the company within the week" (Dalton and Thompson, 1986, p. 88).

To keep in touch with the mainstream of his organization, Alan constantly asks himself questions like:

- Who are the decision makers and the gatekeepers?
- What are people talking about? (What events, values, myths recur in conversation enough to be themes?)
- Who speaks to whom? When? Why?
- What are the status symbols? Who's losing some? Who's gaining some?
- Where is the money going? Who's losing some? Who's gaining some?
- Where is the money coming from?

When talking to management up the line Alan will

- ask for a commitment of time and attention before he begins a conversation. Walter Pruitt may try to do five other things while Alan talks to him. Alan could find himself talking to the wall. So Alan will preface any serious conversation with some request for commitment like, "Walter, I need your full attention for five minutes. When may I have it?"
- *always* be on time. Like many engineers, Walter Pruitt would be annoyed by even a two-minute wait. And Walters' watch is probably set by the official broadcast of UTC (Universal Coordinated Time). Isn't everybody's? So Alan will be there five minutes early. He won't waste that five minutes. He can review his prepared notes while he waits.
- *always* have a notebook and pen with him. If he is asking the questions, he will write them out beforehand and leave space to jot down the answers. If he is offering information, he will have the information outlined and check it off as he discusses it. If Walter makes requests or gives information, Alan will take detailed notes.
- *always* have on the tip of his tongue an executive summary of the status of his project. He will be ready to highlight progress since the last conversation; work remaining; time spent; time remaining; money spent; money left; problems expected; options available; and support needed from management. Alan can provide a one-sentence summary of each item, then provide details as they are requested.
- get to the point quickly. Do what needs to be done and then leave. Alan has heard Walter comment about another employee: "Watching that man work is like watching paint dry." So Alan won't subject Walter to long, tedious, blow-by-blow accounts.
- *never* allow a part of the truth (whatever its source) to paint an inaccurate picture. Many technical people consider that worse than out and out lying. Alan won't avoid facing the whole truth.
- *never* drop a bomb on management—especially in the presence of others. Technical people are typically good problem solvers—if they know about a problem in time. Alan won't delay raising an unpleasant issue hoping it will go away. He will raise it in time for management to do something about it.

SUMMARY

When a project manager plans the interaction, he must take Step A: *Identify the management tools that can contribute most to project success.* His company's experience with project technology, the extent of agreement over project outcomes, and the size of the project will determine which of these four management tools he should emphasize:

- Formal planning
- Formal controls
- External integration
- Internal integration

When a project is **large** and has **well-defined outcomes** but there is only **low company experience** behind it, a project manager should expect to depend heavily on formal planning and control techniques.

When a project has **well-defined outcomes** and **high company experience** behind it, he should expect to draw heavily on internal integration.

When a project is **large** and has only **loosely-defined outcomes** with **low company experience** behind it, he should expect to emphasize external integration, formal planning, and formal control.

When a project has only **loosely defined outcomes** but **high company experience** behind it, the project manager will find his people skills at peak demand. He will rely heavily on external integration and internal integration.

External integration is especially difficult but too costly to ignore. To best use this important tool, the project manager can

- select clients as project team members;
- place clients in key positions on project teams;
- involve clients in key decisions such as approval of specifications and of key action dates;
- clearly define areas of client responsibility (such as management of a change control process, education about a new system, installation of the system);
- communicate formally with other members of the client group;
- communicate systematically with key people in the organization as a whole—as with progress reports to a corporate steering committee.

Choosing The Right Management Tools

Locate the appropriate box for your project on the chart below. Then circle the management tools you expect to be most important to your project success.

- Formal control
- Formal planning
- External integration
- Internal integration

Table 4–3
Management Tools for Project Success

Experience with Technology	Outcomes	
	Loosely-defined Outcomes	Well-defined Outcomes
High Company Experience	Internal Integration External Integration	Internal Integration
Low Company Experience	External Integration Formal Control Formal Planning (if project is large)	Formal Control Formal Planning (if project is large)

Using External Integration

To provide external integration

1. Select clients as project team members. Look for the following:
    * Someone who is technically competent.
    * Someone who is an opinion leader.
    * Someone who has worked with you or with other team members before. (If this isn't possible, look for someone who has a good track record on interdepartmental projects.)

2. Place clients in key positions on project teams.
    * Assign specific roles for each meeting and rotate them: historian, conscience, gatekeeper, time keeper.
    * Let client know role assignment ahead of time.
    * Give client opportunity to represent the team publicly.

3. Involve clients in key decisions such as approval of specifications and key action dates.
    * Distribute agenda.
    * Distribute summary.

4. Clearly define areas of client responsibility.
    * Draft list of client responsibilities.
    * Revise for project agreement.
    * Establish change control procedure.

5. Communicate formally with other members of the client group.
    * Establish contact with key users.
    * Establish contact with every member of the client group who has a responsibility listed in the revised project agreement.

6. Communicate systematically with key people in the organization as a whole.
    * Keep in touch with the mainstream. Listen for answers to questions such as
      —Who are the decision makers and the gatekeepers?
      —What are people talking about? (What events, values, myths recur in conversation enough to be themes?)
      —Who speaks to whom? When? Why?

—What are the status symbols? Who's losing some? Who's gaining some?

—Where is the money going? Who's losing some? Who's gaining some?

—Where is the money coming from?

- When you talk to management

—ask for a commitment of time and attention;

—always be on time;

—always have a notebook and pen;

—always have an executive summary on the tip of your tongue;

—get to the point quickly;

—never allow a part of the truth to paint an inaccurate picture;

—never drop a bomb.

5

*U*sing *I*ntegration *I*ntegration

INTRODUCTION

In a recent survey, technical managers described the characteristics of people they worked with. According to the survey, technical people

". . . are very detail oriented. They want to know details to the nth degree. But they are reluctant to share information themselves."

". . . are less concerned about 'end users.' They don't look at how a product will be used in the 'real world.'"

". . . are 'starters' and not 'finishers' and hate paperwork. They get the work done but they won't document it."

". . . want a lot of freedom and flexibility in doing their jobs."

". . . are high-achievers. Sometimes overachievers."

". . . are antistructural."

". . . like to keep to themselves. They don't have strong people skills."

" . . . are highly opinionated—experts in all fields."

" . . . are thorough and analytical. They can help us see things more systematically."

". . . are loyal to their own professions but *not* to their employer. The source of their paychecks doesn't seem to matter."

". . . can hold you hostage if their priorities don't match the organization's."

And some of the technical management literature is unflattering. One author characterizes the engineer, for example, this way:

". . . hard-nosed, insensitive, goal oriented, unemotional, cold-blooded, demands precision, is self-dependent, impatient with hesitation, and is insistent on getting the job done" (Gibson, 1981, p. 22).

Let's see how the members of Alan's team compare to these stereotypes. First, there's John Redmon, a mechanical engineer. Redmon has another functional supervisor in engineering, but he is reporting to Alan on this project. He has been with Aerodigm since he retired from the army. For a number of years he held a leadership position with the Corps of Engineers. Redmon just doesn't have much faith in computerized systems. Changes in temperature, in hydraulic pressure, in pneumatic pressure—those are things you can rely on. Why depend on a magnetic field that can be disrupted by humidity, by a surge of electricity, or by umpteen other things?

Next, Laney Adams, a computer specialist. Adams came to Aerodigm two years ago—right after graduating with honors from a prestigious university. She's bright and quick and has no patience with anyone who doesn't seem the same. She's so sure of herself, she doesn't really attend to another person's point of view. In a few years, if she mellows, she'd be a great contributor to a team—she has a lot to offer. But right now her sharp edges make her difficult to work with.

Finally, a review of what we know about George Bell, the team member from production. Bell is relatively new at Aerodigm. He doesn't especially like the authoritarian style of his supervisor Mark Johnson. But it's what he's used to. And he doesn't like the brash, surly style of his co-worker Brad Thornton. But he's used to that, too. On the other hand, he does like the more democratic approach to things that seems prevalent in some other divisions. However, he's rather bewildered by it. And when he works with people outside his division, he can't quite figure out which way to go. He keeps Mark Johnson posted on this project work. But—almost 100 percent of the time—when he heads for a project meeting, Johnson will delay him with some trivial questions or with the assignment of some busy work.

At any meeting outside of the company, each of these team members would likely be the soul of decorum: strictly following protocol, not speaking unless spoken to (though they might claim later they "didn't have the opportunity to give input"), fastidiously allowing tempting opportunities for sarcasm to pass without comment. But within Alan's project team, only George Bell maintains the appearance of cooperation. John's bad-mouthing and Laney's abruptness are really keeping Alan on his toes.

Since the team is already in place, Alan will have to make the best of the team composition—at least for the time being. So his use of several of these tools for internal integration will be limited.

- Select experienced technical people to the project team.
- Select team members who have worked together before.
- Select a compatible project manager (or *be* compatible).
- Communicate within the team.
- Involve team members in setting goals and deadlines.
- Get outside technical assistance.

HOW TO USE THE TOOL OF INTERNAL INTEGRATION

Let's see how Alan's team stacks up so far and what tools Alan can still use.

Select experienced technical people to the project team

A project conducted by a technically competent staff may fail if the staff is interpersonally incompetent. But surely almost all would fail if the staff were technically incompetent. As important as interpersonal skills are, they are not a substitute for technical skills. Interpersonal skills are necessary but not sufficient for project success. One extensive study that compared successful projects to projects that failed, ranked technical skills as most important to project success, interpersonal skills as second, and administrative skills as third. These technical characteristics were among those factors with a linear relationship to perceived project success or failure:

- adequate project team capability;
- adequate planning and control techniques;
- adequate initial cost estimates;
- adequate funding to completion (Baker and others, 1983, pp. 671–672).

The only person Alan actually selected to his team was John Redmon; other team members were assigned to him. But each of his project team members is technically competent and experienced. So Alan needn't worry about adequate team capability.

That same technical experience that is so important to project success, however, is likely to make cooperation within the team more difficult to achieve. John Redmon has seen many elaborate computer controls installed—often as a result of slick sales techniques, not as a result of user need. And too often they have cost much more, but performed less effectively, than the older pneumatic systems. Laney Adams is the least experienced team member. But she performed impressively on summer projects while working on her degree. Actually, most of her summer work was more challenging and more complicated than this project will be. In fact, she sees this project as a profound bore. George Bell's experience has, for the most part, been with another company. But the quality of his experience is undisputed. George thinks to himself that they ought to stop *talking* about the new system and *do* something about it. Because his team so well satisfies the criteria of technical experience, Alan will call on the other tools at his disposal extensively.

Select team members who have worked together before

Some studies of aircraft incidents suggest that risk is increased by the bidding systems many airlines use. Under the bidding systems, flight crews are often composed of members who have not previously worked together. Even if each individual member is competent, no member knows the strengths and weaknesses of the others. Nor does anyone know the personality traits of the others. By the time a crew member knows whether to expect polish or awkwardness, literal orders or sarcasm, seriousness or fooling around, it's time for reassignment. Some believe the failure to interpret another crew member's behavior accurately has been deadly. They recommend that the bidding system be curtailed (Burrows, 1983, p. 47).

That Alan's team members have never worked together before isn't likely to be deadly. But it could be costly. One of the most difficult problems facing a team composed of strangers is distinguishing between the *information* in a message and the *command* in that message. Suppose an angry father exclaims, "Any idiot can make a decent grade in conduct!" His son is likely to correctly interpret the message as a command: "Don't get a low grade in conduct again!" He's not likely to think his father is simply sharing information. But how are team members likely to hear Alan's message: "We should calibrate the controls against actual conditions"? John is likely to hear the comment as simple confirmation of established fact. Laney has such confidence in automation that she may hear it as an uninformed opinion. George is the only team member likely to hear Alan's message as an assignment. And even he won't know who's expected to do it—nor is he likely to ask.

Another difficult problem facing a team of strangers is the interpretation of humor. A remark such as, "I wouldn't touch that with a ten-foot pole" is subject to several interpretations. One person may hear it as a crack and ignore it. Another may hear an expression of frustration about an unavoidable task. But another could hear it as a command to leave an unpleasant task undone. Sarcasm can be especially difficult for team members to manage. Some may take a sarcastic remark literally. Others may find it a turn off. When a team member offered the suggestion, "If we could manufacture this component ourselves, we could save a lot," his project manager snapped "If frogs could fly, they wouldn't have to drag their tails through the mud!" The team member dropped the idea which could have saved the company substantial dollars.

Alan can help minimize both these problems by being explicit about his expectations. He can be explicit about specific assignments. When he wants an individual to do a particular thing, he can say so in no uncertain terms: whom he expects to do what and when. He can be explicit about group roles and gauge his own behavior accordingly. He can invite team suggestions and questions. Then he can reward the suggestions and questions when they come, not shut them off with sarcasm.

Select a compatible project manager

In this case, Alan must *be* the compatible project manager if his project is to succeed. To a great extent, he will need to adjust to each team member's personal style in order to get full value from that person's participation. Since John is the only team member he has known previously, Alan will make a special effort to *be there,* to *listen,* and to *respond with respect.*

Alan will be sure he has some informal time alone with each team member—daily if possible. That may mean he comes in early some days because he knows Laney will be there having a cup of coffee and Danish before she starts work. It may mean he stops off at The Boar's Head on Thursday where he knows George stops for a drink. It may mean he brings his lunch one day so he can eat at one of the picnic tables by the lake as John does.

It's tempting for a group leader to do the talking when he's with his team members. Leadership has been stereotyped as "giving orders and giving advice." The sense of power that comes with giving orders and the sense of wisdom that comes with giving advice feed that stereotype. But in one study, listening was among the seven top factors that distinguished managers of successful projects from managers of projects that failed (Hill, 1977, pp. 45–61). Alan will make a point of spending most of his time with team members listening, not talking. During his listening time he will carefully avoid giving orders and giving advice; he will resist the temptation to inject war stories or to engage in one-upmanship. He will simply listen.

Alan may have a mouthful to say in response. (That has often been the case when Laney has erupted in a vitriolic attack on another employee.) But before he introduces his own reaction, he will first show the team member he has listened. First, he will count to ten after a team member has spoken to be sure there's no more to come. Next, he will briefly summarize in his own words what the team member has said. Then he'll get confirmation from the team member that he has correctly understood before he proceeds.

Because he has been there, listened, and responded with respect, Alan has already learned a great deal about his team members who were total strangers such a short time ago. John's negativism is a little easier to take now that Alan realizes it stems in part from fear of being replaced by "a bunch of new-fangled" equipment. Laney's abrasiveness is a little less grating now that Alan has heard her fears about "making it in the real world." George's tentativeness is a little less exasperating now that Alan knows about Mark Johnson's interference with George's project time.

Communicate within the team

Significant communication within Alan's team will go on during project meetings. But he will not ignore other opportunities for developing and maintaining good communication with team members.

Project meetings are notorious targets for endless complaints: they last too long, they don't accomplish anything, they steal time from the real work, they're just used to c.y.a., and on and on. Unfortunately the complaints are often justified. But Alan has developed some rules of thumb over the years to ensure his project meetings count. He will be careful to do the following:

- Use many of the same communication techniques with other team members that he has used with his client member, George: He will rotate roles, distribute an agenda, provide meeting summaries which include key action items and key decisions.
- Meet at the right intervals. What is right in this case? Alan met daily with his team during the first week of its existence. He felt that daily meetings were important until the team established priorities, agreed on a schedule, and developed administrative procedures. Now some critical technical issues have surfaced. To be sure they don't block team performance, Alan has scheduled meetings twice a week until they are resolved. He believes they can be cleared up in a couple of weeks. Thereafter, the team can meet just weekly and still adequately exchange and update information. (If the project were of longer duration, every other week might be enough.) When the project is phasing out, the intervals will probably be shortened to twice a week for a couple of weeks and then daily for a while.
- Meet on the right day and at the right time. At the very beginning of the project meeting dates and times were agreed upon: Daily at 8:00 a.m. through the organizational phases (estimated one week); on Tuesdays and Thursdays at 8:00 a.m. until technical disagreements were cleared up (estimated two additional weeks); Thursdays at 8:00 a.m. until further notice. And throughout the project, Alan will consider the 8:00 to 10:00 a.m. time slot inviolable. He

will not give his team the impression that this project is less important than other commitments by switching the time around to accommodate other activities (unless there is a decreed company-wide activity over which he has no control).

- Meet at the right location. The right location is not just a logical choice—it's a psychological one. Since Alan and John are both in the engineering group, their departmental conference room would be a logical choice. But it would be a poor psychological choice. Both George and Laney would have to travel some distance to get there. And George would have the added nuisance of checking in and out of a separate security area. Besides, Alan and John would be vulnerable to phone calls and other interruptions as long as they stayed in their area. So Alan will arrange to use a conference room in the administration building. Each team member will travel about the same distance to get there, no one will need to check through security, and no one will be convenient to interruptions.

- Alan will see to it that the conference room is furnished to meet team needs. Since he will encourage team members to use visual aids, he will be sure the room has both an overhead projector and an easel stand. Since each team member will be referring to wiring diagrams, he will be sure each person has fifteen to twenty square feet of table surface.

- Seek consensus. Alan wouldn't choose to be a dictator. But in a technical project "putting it to a vote" doesn't often make sense either. Alan will work for agreement on action items and decisions. Ironically, to reach agreement he must air *dis*agreements rather than squelch them. He must explore alternatives rather than push for linear progress.

Whether in a project meeting or out, Alan will look for opportunities to give his team members support. He will accept full responsibility to top management for problems. But he will give credit for breakthroughs to the team. He will pass on compliments he hears and add his own. When compliments are scarce, he will make contact with each team member just to see how things are going.

Alan will consistently be honest with team members. He won't whitewash the problems at Aerodigm; he will acknowledge them truthfully. But neither will he burden his team with bad-mouthing or "poor me-ism."

Involve team members in setting goals and deadlines

Alan will be sure to involve other team members as he does the client member. He will let each member know what action items and decisions he expects to surface. He will summarize action items and decisions after they have been agreed upon.

Get outside technical assistance

Outside help is especially important under two conditions: (1) when things aren't going well at all and (2) when things are going too well. When things aren't going well at all, an outsider can offer a fresh point of view on a technical issue. Or he can play the mediator's role in an interpersonal conflict. When things are going too well, an outsider can help the group think critically and avoid a bad decision. Too well? That's right. When a group really "clicks," team members may stifle their own opinions in order to promote group cohesiveness. (That tendency is called groupthink.) As a result a pharmaceutical firm may release a drug that should be tested further. A manufacturer may produce an automobile with a deadly design flaw. A corporation may adopt a strategy that ignores its market.

In case Alan's group gets stuck or bends toward groupthink, Alan has a list of outside resources in mind. One could be a guest facilitator if feelings run high, over time, in project meetings. One is an old-time technical specialist who has actually enjoyed the onset of computerization. One has been the project director of several plant renovations. In some situations, Alan might be able to call on an outsider from another division. In some cases the outsider might be with another company. What if internal politics preclude the use of a resource from another division? And confidentiality precludes the use of a resource from another company? Then Alan can draw on the skills of a reputable consultant—one who is technically competent and who will maintain confidentiality.

SUMMARY

A project manager begins to plan the interaction by taking Step A: *Identify the management tools that contribute most to project success.* Under some circumstances, the tool of internal integration will be critical. When a project has **well-defined outcomes** and **high company experience** behind it, the project manager should expect to draw heavily on internal integration.

When a project has only **loosely defined outcomes** but **high company experience** behind it, the project manager will find his people skills at peak demand. He will rely heavily on external integration and internal integration.

To best use the tool of internal integration, the project manager can

- select experienced technical people to the project team;
- select team members who have worked together before;
- select a compatible project manager (or *be* compatible);
- communicate within the team;
- involve team members in setting goals and deadlines;
- get outside technical assistance.

Providing Internal Integration

To provide internal integration:

1. Select experienced technical people to the project team.

2. Select team members who have worked together before. If that's not possible look for people with good track records on interdepartmental projects and
   • Be explicit about specific assignments;
   • Be explicit about group roles.

3. Select a compatible project manager (or *be* one!):
   • be there;
   • listen;
   • respond with respect.

4. Communicate within the team.
   • rotate roles;
   • distribute an agenda;
   • provide meeting summaries;
   • meet at the right intervals;
   • meet on the right day and at the right time;
   • meet at the right location;
   • seek consensus;
   • give support;
     —accept responsibility for problems;
     —give credit to team;
     —pass on compliments and add your own;
     —stay in touch;
   • be honest but not negative.

5. Involve team members in setting goals and deadlines:
   • provide agenda that includes action items and decisions you expect to surface;
   • provide summary including action items and decisions agreed upon.

6. Get outside technical assistance if
   • things are not going well at all;
   • things are going too well.

6

*S*peaking *P*lainly, *U*nderstanding *C*learly

INTRODUCTION

"Here's to plain speaking and clear understandings."

It was the villain (played by Sidney Greenstreet) in the *Maltese Falcon* who raised this toast. He recognized the value of honest, uncluttered communication even though his vocation made that kind of communication difficult—even unlikely. Like Greenstreet's character, most project managers recognize the value of honest, uncluttered communication. And their vocations, too, make that kind of communication difficult, even unlikely.

In the first place, many of us have the nagging feeling that although the uncluttered truth is the best choice in most cases, it somehow won't work in this situation. We somehow won't be able to pull it off this time without the help of some elaboration. But we can take heart from the instances, time after time, when honesty and simplicity have won out.

One such instance was the 1857 lawsuit brought by the owner of the *Effie Afton* against the Railroad Bridge Company. When the steampship *Effie Afton* ran into a bridge support and caught fire, steamshippers had the excuse they wanted to claim that railroad bridges (aids to east-west transportation) were an immoral hazard.

Arguments were detailed and lengthy on both sides. But many said the vindication of the Railroad Bridge Company was insured by lawyer Abraham Lincoln's one-liner:

"One man has as good a right to cross a river as another has to sail up or down it" (Woldeman, 1936, p. 172).

Lincoln clearly understood the real issue beneath the rhetoric. And his plain speaking gave it power.

But the power of the uncluttered truth can raise a second barrier. Many of us associate power with anger—with being either victim or villain. Fortunately, there is an alternative: taking care of ourselves without victimizing anyone else.

The last chapter helped the project manager complete Step A: select the most useful management tools for the interaction his project would require. This chapter can help the project manager

- uncover and understand the real issues and
- speak them plainly without anger.

To meet the goals you should continue to plan the interaction by following these remaining steps:

Step B. *Visualize key people and their location across boundaries in your organization.*

Step C. *Analyze conflicting pressures in the organization and the impact the project (or an idea) will have on them.*

Step D. *Build key elements into a negotiation plan.*

Step E. *Organize what you know about key people and the interaction among them to get an edge on personality conflict.*

Step F. *Build a win-win presentation into your negotiation style.*

◆ Step B ◆

VISUALIZE KEY PEOPLE AND THEIR LOCATION ACROSS BOUNDARIES IN THE ORGANIZATION

The requirement to cross boundaries in an organization is a strong predictor of one stress producer—role conflict (Miles, 1976, p. 177; Miles and Perrault, 1976, p. 31). And stress increases the likelihood of communication breakdown. Carl Rogers says it well:

". . . the stronger our feelings the more likely it is that there will be no mutual element in the communication. There will be just two ideas, two feelings, two judgments, missing each other in psychological space" (Rogers, 1961, p. 331).

In fact, when a project manager must communicate across two or more boundaries in an organization, he should expect to *translate* in order to get his point across. Whether boundaries separate technologies or levels of decision making, they also separate languages. A person's language is shaped by his view of the world (and vice versa). And his view of the world can be shaped by the view from his place of work.

To get a clear picture of how boundaries in an organization affect key people, a project manager can:

1. list key people;
2. identify the technology of each key person;
3. rank order the technologies by degree of abstractness;
4. place each key person on an organizational pyramid scaled to visualize the depth and span of the project.

List key people

In each project and for special situations within each project, the manager should consider at least five categories of people. The decision maker, the opinion leader, the gatekeeper, the client, and other team members. And on some projects there are two additional categories: big brothers (government regulatory agencies) and little brothers (company regulatory committees or officials). As we define the categories, we'll identify the key people for Alan Lord's project as a whole.

The decision maker is the person who can say (and make it stick) "Yes" or "No," "Go" or "No go," "This project has succeeded," or

"This project has failed." Sometimes the decision maker is the client, but often it is someone in the project manager's own chain of command. In Alan's project, the client is a hostile one who is likely to dub the project a failure no matter what. But the project was actually authorized by the vice-president for science and engineering, Edward Dalton. Ultimately, if Dalton says the project has succeeded, the project has succeeded. Situation by situation, Alan will try to solve problems at the lowest level possible. But he will list Dalton as the decision maker for the project as a whole.

The opinion leader is the person whose recommendation the decision maker is likely to accept. Sometimes the decision maker is influenced by a secretary or by a golf buddy. Alan knows of no such influential person with Dalton. Sometimes the decision maker relies on the official recommendation of someone in the chain of command. In this project, Dalton is keenly aware of the personal rivalry between Alan's supervisor (Walter Pruitt) and the client (Mark Johnson). Dalton is likely to take the recommendation of either one with a grain of salt. Alan can't identify the opinion leader for this project. So he may cultivate a position of influence with Dalton himself.

The gatekeeper is the person who controls the flow of information between the project manager and the decision maker. In Alan's case, he cannot reach Ed Dalton initially without going through Walter Pruitt. Walter, then, is the gatekeeper.

The client is the person who will use the product or the service that results from the project. In this project, Mark Johnson is the client. Ironically, Johnson himself may not want the project to succeed. It is not safe to assume that the people who could benefit from a project are, in fact, supporters of it.

Team members are those who are officially designated to work on the project. In this case team members are Alan Lord (project manager), John Redmon, Laney Adams, and George Bell.

Big brothers are the government regulators that may intervene. On large, external projects the list could seem endless: Occupational Health and Safety Administration (OSHA), the Equal Employment Opportunity Commission (EEOC), the Environmental Protection Agency (EPA), the State Department of Labor (DOL), and many others. Sometimes a representative of one of these agencies may have a hidden agenda. And perhaps there's a slim chance it would be "easier to get forgiveness than permission." But the cost of guessing wrong could be high. So the project manager should designate responsible people on his team to get current on what is expected by each big brother before the team reaches the drawing table. Even in Alan's internal project, the plant control systems that result will be inspected by the county electrical inspector, the fire department, and EPA. So Alan will specify a team member to double-check code in each of these categories.

Little brothers are the company regulatory committees. They could include a health officer, an EEO Committee, a corporate governance board, and a variety of others. In this project, Alan will get input from the health officer early on.

Table 6-1 shows Alan's list of key people.

Identify the technology of each key person

The number of technologies represented on a project is one predictor of the number of languages the project manager must speak. Table 6-2 shows Alan's list with the technologies added.

Rank order the technologies by degree of abstractness

How do technical boundaries line up? The engineer stereotype is a person who sees every issue as "all or nothing," "black or white." The physicist stereotype is of a Renaissance man, someone who knows a lot about a lot. The psychologist stereotype is the "absentminded professor" who bungles practical tasks. Like other occupational stereotypes, these have their roots in the extent to which an occupation requires hands-on performance of concrete tasks as opposed to abstract thinking. Of course, stereotypes don't hold up individual by individual; but it's true that the abstractness or concreteness of a person's work is likely to color his view of the world. The aircraft technician who actually handles components will see the craft differently from the design engineer who will work more with symbols for those components. And the odds are they will see the world differently too. So lining up technical areas by degree of abstractness is one good way to visualize the number of boundaries a project manager must cross.

Table 6-3 shows how the technologies in Alan's project line up. He has left the rank of "0" for most concrete unassigned. That rank would go to staff in the personnel core of the organization.

Table 6–1
Alan's List of Key People

1. LIST KEY PEOPLE.
Official Decision Maker (DM) *Edward Dalton* *(V.P. Science & Engineering)*
Opinion Leader (OL) *Me?* *(Project Manager)*
Gatekeeper (G) *Walter Pruitt* *(My Supervisor)*
Client (C) *Mark Johnson*
Team Member$_1$ (TM$_1$) *Me* *(Project Manager)*
Team Member$_2$ (TM$_2$) *John Redmon*
Team Member$_3$ (TM$_3$) *Laney Adams*
Team Member$_4$ (TM$_4$) *George Bell*
Team Member$_5$ (TM$_5$) *Big Brothers and Little Brothers*

Table 6–2
Alan's List with the Technologies Added

1. LIST KEY PEOPLE.	2. IDENTIFY TECHNOLOGY.
Official Decision Maker (DM) *Edward Dalton* *(V.P. Science & Engineering)*	*Engineering Mgt.*
Opinion Leader (OL) *Me?* *(Project Manager)*	*Elect. Engineer*
Gatekeeper (G) *Walter Pruitt* *(My Supervisor)*	*Engineering Mgt.*
Client (C) Mark Johnson	*Production Mgt.*
Team Member$_1$ (TM$_1$) *Me* *(Project Manager)*	*Elect. Engineer*
Team Member$_2$ (TM$_2$) *John Redmon*	*Mech. Engineer*
Team Member$_3$ (TM$_3$) *Laney Adams*	*Computer Spec.*
Team Member$_4$ (TM$_4$) *George Bell*	*Production Sup.*
Team Member$_5$ (TM$_5$) *Big Brothers and Little Brothers*	

Table 6–3
Alan's List with Technologies Rank Ordered

1. LIST KEY PEOPLE.	2. IDENTIFY TECHNOLOGY.	3. RANK. (0 = concrete x = very abstract)
Official Decision Maker (DM) Edward Dalton (V.P. Science & Engineering)	Engineering Mgt.	3
Opinion Leader (OL) Me? (Project Manager)	Elect. Engineer	3
Gatekeeper (G) Walter Pruitt (My Supervisor)	Engineering Mgt.	3
Client (C) Mark Johnson	Production Mgt.	1
Team Member$_1$ (TM$_1$) Me (Project Manager)	Elect. Engineer	3
Team Member$_2$ (TM$_2$) John Redmon	Mech. Engineer	2
Team Member$_3$ (TM$_3$) Laney Adams	Computer Spec.	4
Team Member$_4$ (TM$_4$) George Bell	Production Sup.	1
Team Member$_5$ (Tm$_5$) Big Brothers and Little Brothers		0–99

Place each key person on an organizational pyramid scaled to visualize the depth and span of the project

Decision making levels scale the depth of a project, technical areas the span. When these elements are plotted on an organizational pyramid, they can help a project manager visualize the communication barriers he will face. Alan's pyramid looks like this.

Figure 6–1
Alan's Organizational Pyramid

4. Now place each key person on an organizational pyramid to visualize the depth and span of your project.

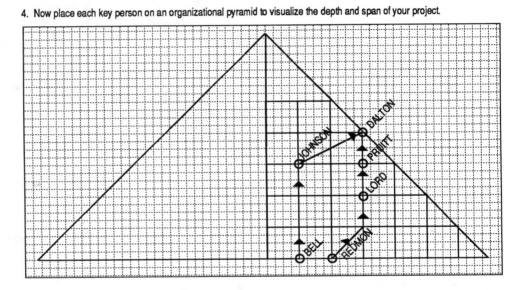

But Alan's drawing of the pyramid is only an aid. The real visual is in his head. That's where he sees the line between electrical engineering and computer services as a very thin one and the line between mechanical engineering and production as a chasm. Alan's mental picture yields much richer information than the simple, two-dimensional drawing.

◆ Step C ◆ ANALYZE CONFLICTING PRESSURES IN THE ORGANIZATION AND THE IMPACT THE PROJECT (OR AN IDEA) WILL HAVE ON THEM

Roles will vary from situation to situation throughout a project. But an analysis of any particular situation is a temporary overlay of the analysis for the project as a whole. Table 6-4 shows how Alan analyzed the impact of his project as a whole.

Table 6–4

Step B–1: LIST KEY PEOPLE.	Step B–2: IDENTIFY TECHNOLOGY.	Step B–3: RANK. [0 = concrete . . . x = very abstract]	Step C: **ANALYZE IMPACT**
Official Decision Maker (DM) *Edward Dalton (V.P. Science & Engineering)*	*Engineering Mgt.*	*3*	**Could end at least this skirmish in the ongoing feud between Johnson and Pruitt. In fact, the project could help clarify who's the bad guy and who's the good guy.**
Opinion Leader (OL) *Me? (Project Manager)*	*Elect. Engineer*	*3*	**Would mean I get to do something else. (What a relief that would be!)**
Gatekeeper (G) *Walter Pruitt (My Supervisor)*	*Engineering Mgt.*	*3*	**Would satisfy Dalton. Might show Dalton that Pruitt is not instigator of trouble with Johnson. Might shut Johnson up.**
Client (C) *Mark Johnson*	*Production Mgt.*	*1*	**Would make him lose this skirmish with in battle with Pruitt. Could make Pruitt look good.**

Table 6–4
continued

Team Member₁ (TM₁) *Me* *(Project Manager)*	*Elect. Engineer*	3	**Would get this mess over with!**
Team Member₂ (TM₂) *John Redmon*	*Mech. Engineer*	2	**Could force him to admit some value in automated controls.**
Team Member₃ (TM₃) *Laney Adams*	*Computer Spec.*	4	**Could mean she's free to go on to a more interesting project. Could mean she'd need to revise view of project value.**
Team Member₄ (TM₄) *George Bell*	*Production Sup.*	1	**Might cause Johnson to blame him for putting a feather in Pruitt's cap.**
Team Member₅ (TM₅) *Big Brothers and Little Brothers*		0–99	**(This group will need individual analysis.)**

Because of his analysis, he wasn't taken off guard as the problem with George's attendance unfolded. Alan is trying to solve that problem at the lowest possible level first.

- In his first attempt, he approached George as the decision maker. But he soon found out that George wasn't free to decide to be on time: Mark Johnson was requiring George to do things that made George late.
- Now he will approach Mark Johnson as decision maker with George as gatekeeper.
- If his approach to Mark fails, he may still define Mark as the decision maker a second time—this time with Walter Pruitt as gatekeeper.
- But if this attempt fails as well, then he will fall back on his overall project analysis. The vice-president of science and engineering is the ultimate decision maker. He authorized the project and he approved the project plan—including time commitments. If Alan feels Mark Johnson is not honoring those commitments to the extent that the project is in danger, he will approach the vice-president as decision maker with Walter as gatekeeper.

Why not just let it drift? Alan is in the strongest position to deal with the problem at the very beginning. As he invested more time, energy, and ego in the project, he would be more vulnerable to Mark Johnson's lack of support. The temptation would grow to avoid the hassle with Mark and just do more and more himself to compensate for George's absences. Kepler's Third Law would likely prevail: Alan would travel faster and faster in smaller and smaller circles. With an apparently hostile client, Alan's only hope to thwart Kepler's Third Law lies in his ability and willingness to say "No" from the very beginning.

Let's apply the remaining steps of Alan's analysis to his current attempt to deal with Mark Johnson. Here's what his analysis of this individual situation would look like so far:

Table 6–5
Alan's Analysis of the Attendance Problem

Step B–1: LIST KEY PEOPLE.	Step B–2: IDENTIFY TECHNOLOGY.	Step B–3: RANK. [0 = concrete x = very abstract]	Step C: ANALYZE IMPACT
Official Decision Maker (DM) *Mark Johnson*	*Production Mgt.*	*1*	**Would forfeit one opportunity to thwart Walter Pruitt's staff.**
Opinion Leader (OL)			
Gatekeeper (G) *George Bell*	*Production Sup.*	*1*	**Might require an unpleasant encounter with Johnson.** **Might catch him in middle of conflict between Johnson and Pruitt.** **Could free him to be at project meetings on time.**
Client (C)			
Team Member$_1$ (TM$_1$) *Me*	*Elect. Engineer*	*3*	**Could allow me to start project meetings on time with all members present. Could get me caught in middle of a lot of unpleasantness.**
Team Member$_2$ (TM$_2$)			

◆ Step D ◆ BUILD KEY ELEMENTS INTO A NEGOTIATION PLAN

We're used to thinking of stakes in a project as dollar amounts. But dollars aren't a project manager's only negotiable currency. Research shows that people are more likely to invest a change in their own behavior when they are assured of certain conditions. When he approaches George as gatekeeper, Alan will

1. collaborate with George in setting goals for an agreement with Mark;
2. consult George beforehand about the parameters of a meeting with Mark;
3. enlist support for George;
4. negotiate for the autonomy George needs;
5. reinforce George's efforts after the fact.

Figure 6-2 shows Alan's notes about the currency for negotiation with George.

◆ Step E ◆ ORGANIZE WHAT YOU KNOW ABOUT KEY PEOPLE AND THE INTERACTION BETWEEN THEM TO GET AN EDGE ON PERSONALITY CONFLICT

Most project managers have many tidbits of information about their team members floating around in their heads. These tidbits can be much more useful if they are organized visually to show what opposition can be expected and what support can be expected.

Figure 6-3 shows how Alan organizes what he knows about George as he prepares to talk to George as gatekeeper.

◆ Step F ◆ BUILD A WIN-WIN PRESENTATION INTO YOUR NEGOTIATION STYLE

In 1557 Queen Elizabeth I wanted to buy a tract of land from the church to give to a gentleman friend for a garden. When she asked a bishop about it, he told her he would not sell. Then she wrote him this handy little note quoted in its entirety on page 75.

Figure 6–2
Alan's Notes for Negotiating with George as Gatekeeper

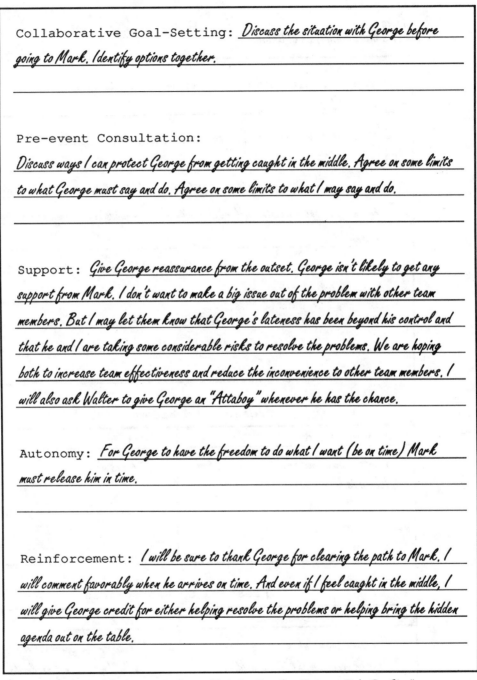

Collaborative Goal-Setting: *Discuss the situation with George before going to Mark. Identify options together.*

Pre-event Consultation:

Discuss ways I can protect George from getting caught in the middle. Agree on some limits to what George must say and do. Agree on some limits to what I may say and do.

Support: *Give George reassurance from the outset. George isn't likely to get any support from Mark. I don't want to make a big issue out of the problem with other team members. But I may let them know that George's lateness has been beyond his control and that he and I are taking some considerable risks to resolve the problems. We are hoping both to increase team effectiveness and reduce the inconvenience to other team members. I will also ask Walter to give George an "Attaboy" whenever he has the chance.*

Autonomy: *For George to have the freedom to do what I want (be on time) Mark must release him in time.*

Reinforcement: *I will be sure to thank George for clearing the path to Mark. I will comment favorably when he arrives on time. And even if I feel caught in the middle, I will give George credit for either helping resolve the problems or helping bring the hidden agenda out on the table.*

Based on House, Ruth Sizemore. "Increase Training Benefits: Decrease Role Conflict," Performance and Instruction, 21, 5, pp. 14–15.

Figure 6–3
Alan's Market Analysis of George

☐ The Official Decision-Maker: _____

☐ The Opinion Leader: _____

☒ The Gatekeeper: *George* _____

☐ The Consumer: _____

Personal Style: *Unsure of himself and his role. Put off by his supervisor's brash style but not quite comfortable with more openness in two-way communication either.*

Relationship with You: *Good so far — but it's still an uncertain relationship.*

Relationships with Other Key People: *George is wary of his supervisor. He has no real relationship established with other team members yet.*

Pressure to Accept Idea

Job-Related	Other
* *Wants to be a good project team member.* * *Wants to be on time.*	* *Likes me.*

Pressure to Resist Idea

Job-Related	Other
* *Pressure from Johnson.* * *Fear of being caught in the middle.* * *Concern about job security.*	* *Unassertive personal style.* * *Would rather not deal with Johnson.*

Proud Prelate, you know what you were before I made you what you are today. If you do not immediately comply with my request, I will unfrock you. By God.

Elizabeth
(Linton, 1962, p. 89)

Now Elizabeth had line authority. And she didn't seem to be worried about having a good working relationship with the church official two weeks later. Or a year later. Or ever, for that matter.

But project managers often don't have line authority over people whose compliance they want. And more often than not, the person they are in conflict with today is someone they will still be working with two weeks later or a year later. So it is the practical project manager as well as the humanitarian one who takes care of his project without unnecessarily harming other people—even when he needs to get tough.

Alan will review what he knows about George to plan his course of action. And he will build much of what he knows into an actual script for his conversation with George.

George's strongest job-related pressure to resist Alan's conversation with Mark is that he doesn't want to get caught in the middle—he doesn't want to say "No" or seem insubordinate to the person who appraises his work and approves his pay voucher. Alan will acknowledge this pressure to show he understands the risks to George. (See "Empathy Statement" in Figure 6-4.)

George's strongest job-related pressure to support Alan's conversation with Mark is that he wants to be a good team member. He doesn't want to waste the time of the other members. Alan will include this pressure in his statement of the problem. (See "Statement of the Problem" in Figure 6-5.)

George has several nonjob related pressures which Alan may not address directly. But he will try to accommodate them in the course of action he proposes. (See "Conclusion" in Figure 6-4.)

And using the same process, he has developed the script for his conversation with Mark shown in Figure 6-5.

And if his conversation with Mark fails to get results, he already has decided what he will say to Walter Pruitt (see Figure 6-6).

Figure 6–4
Alan's Script for Conversation with George

Key Person *Gatekeeper: George Bell*

Empathy Statement

George, I understand you're doing your best to get to project meetings on time. And you're embarrassed that it hasn't worked out. Mark has called on you a number of mornings to do something else; you just don't feel you can tell him no.

Connecting Word

But...

Statement of Problem as You See It

...your late arrivals are costing other team members wasted time. As we get further into the project, lost time will hurt more and more. And your input as a team member is too important for us simply to go on without you.

Connecting Word

So...

Conclusion (request, call for action, decision)

...I'd like your support in raising the issue with Mark.

* You can let him know we've had a problem. Then ask him to give you the OK to come directly here without reporting to your work station on days we have project meetings.

* You can let him know we've had a problem and I will be dropping by to talk to him about it.

Or

* I can just call directly for an appointment.

Either way, we will handle the problem without getting you caught in the middle. Mark promised to release your time in our project agreement. We can use that agreement as the basis for our discussion.

Based on Winship, Barbara and Kelley, Jan: "A Verbal Response Model of Assertiveness," Journal of Counseling Psychology, 23, pp. 215–220.

Figure 6–5
Alan's Script for Conversation with Mark

Key Person   *Decision Maker: Mark Johnson*

Empathy Statement

Mark, I understand you like George to report to his work station in the mornings before he comes over to our project meetings. That way he can check to see what calls have come in and what problems came up on the night shift.

Connecting Word

But...

Statement of Problem as You See It

...George needs to leave this building by 7:45 a.m. in order to get to our project meetings on time. He's been late three times when you've given him early morning assignments that kept him here after that time. We just can't afford to keep three people waiting for him. And his input is too important for us to proceed without him

Connecting Word

So...

Conclusion (request, call for action, decision)

...I'd like your renewed commitment of George's time to the project. Will you either

     1. Be sure he is free to leave the building at 7:45 a.m.

Or

     2. Release him to come directly to the project meeting without reporting to his work station first. If necessary we'll begin the meetings at 7:30 instead of 8:00 to match George's duty hours.

Figure 6-6
Alan's Script for Conversation with Walter

Key Person _Gatekeeper: Walter Pruitt_

Empathy Statement

Walter, I realize that the less you have to do with Mark Johnson, the better you like it.
Your dealings with him have been consistently unpleasant. Besides, you're angry that he's
called the v.p.'s attention to the conflict between you.

Connecting Word

But...

Statement of Problem as You See It

...if I leave you out of the picture, I'm afraid he'll be calling the v.p.'s attention to the
failure of this project. Johnson has given George Bell last minute assignments several
times that have made George late for project meetings. I asked Mark to either accept
responsibility for George's being on time or give George the okay to come directly to
project meetings in the morning without reporting to his work station first. Mark said "No"
to both requests. Unless we stand firm on the project agreement now, I expect things to get
worse not better.

Connecting Word

_So..._

Conclusion (request, call for action, decision)

...I'd like your help in one of two ways. Please either

    Talk to Mark yourself

_Or_

    Make me an appointment to see Ed Dalton. We'll look bad unless he understands
now that project success is impossible without Bell's time.

Based on Winship, Barbara and Kelley, Jan: "A Verbal Response Model of Assertiveness," Journal of Counseling Psychology, 23, pp. 215–220.

SUMMARY

After he has selected the management tools for the interaction his project requires (Step A), the project manager must proceed to

- uncover the real issues for key people;
- speak those issues plainly but without anger.

These remaining steps can help.

B. Visualize key people and their locations across boundaries in the organization. Whether the boundaries separate technologies or levels of decision making, they also separate languages. So the project manager must translate as well as communicate.

C. Analyze conflicting pressures in the organization and the impact the project (or an idea) will have on them. A project may have some negative impact even on the client. A quick analysis of impact can prepare the project manager for inherent resistance.

D. Build key elements into a negotiation plan. A key person is more likely to cooperate when the project manager offers collaboration about goals; consultation over parameters; moral support; needed autonomy; and reinforcement.

E. Organize what is known about key people and the interaction between them to get an edge on personality conflict. If they are organized visually, little tidbits of information about key people can show what support and what opposition are likely.

F. Build a win-win presentation into the negotiation style. A practical project manager (not just the humanitarian one) takes care of his project without unnecessarily harming others. His script begins with a statement of the other person's point of view.

Visualizing People

Use the following chart to

1. list key people;
2. identify the technology of each key person;
3. rank order the technology by degree of abstractness;
4. place each key person on an organizational pyramid scaled to visualize the depth and the span of the project.

Analysis Chart: People and Pressures

1. **List Key People**	2. **Identify Technology**	3. **Rank** [0 = concrete x = very abstract]	
Official Decision Maker (DM)			
Opinion Leader (OL)			
Gatekeeper (G)			
Client (C)			
Team Member$_1$ (TM$_1$)			
Team Member$_2$ (TM$_2$)			
Team Member$_3$ (TM$_3$)			
Team Member$_4$ (TM$_4$)			
Team Member$_5$ (TM$_5$)			

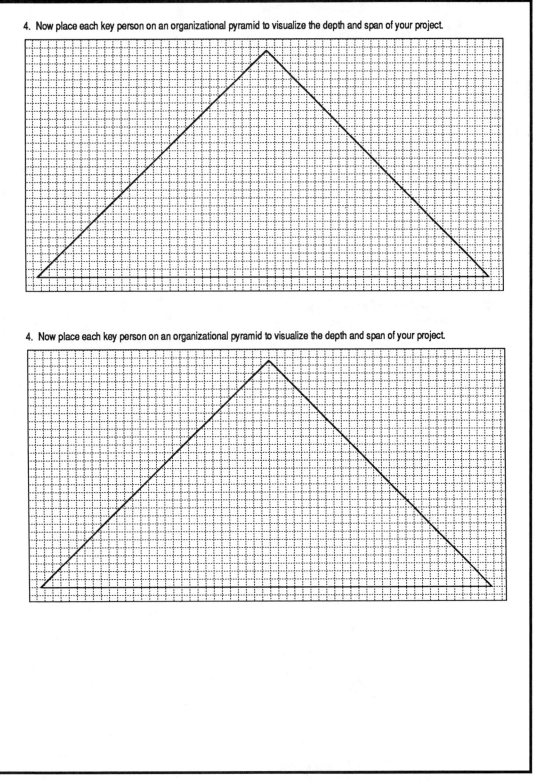

4. Now place each key person on an organizational pyramid to visualize the depth and span of your project.

4. Now place each key person on an organizational pyramid to visualize the depth and span of your project.

Analyzing Pressures

Use the far right column of the same chart to note the impact of your project on each key individual.

Analysis Chart: People and Pressures

1. **List Key People**	2. **Identify Technology**	3. **Rank** [0 = concrete x = very abstract]	**Note Impact**
Official Decision Maker (DM)			
Opinion Leader (OL)			
Gatekeeper (G)			
Client (C)			
Team Member$_1$ (TM$_1$)			
Team Member$_2$ (TM$_2$)			
Team Member$_3$ (TM$_3$)			
Team Member$_4$ (TM$_4$)			
Team Member$_5$ (TM$_5$)			

Building a Negotiation Plan

Use the following worksheets to plan ways you can

1. collaborate in setting goals;
2. consult before a critical event to set parameters;
3. provide moral support;
4. secure the autonomy for each team member to do what needs to be done;
5. reinforce each person's effort to do what you want.

Notes for Negotiating

Collaborative Goal-Setting: _____
_____
_____
_____

Pre-event Consultation:
_____
_____
_____
_____

Support: _____
_____
_____
_____
_____
_____

Autonomy:_____
_____
_____
_____

Reinforcement: _____
_____
_____
_____

Notes for Negotiating

Collaborative Goal-Setting: _____

_____

_____

_____

Pre-event Consultation: _____

_____

_____

_____

_____

Support: _____

_____

_____

_____

_____

_____

Autonomy: _____

_____

_____

_____

Reinforcement: _____

_____

_____

_____

Notes for Negotiating

Collaborative Goal-Setting: _____

_____

_____

_____

Pre-event Consultation: _____

_____

_____

_____

_____

Support: _____

_____

_____

_____

_____

_____

_____

Autonomy: _____

_____

_____

_____

Reinforcement: _____

_____

_____

_____

Notes for Negotiating

Collaborative Goal-Setting: _____

_____

_____

_____

Pre-event Consultation:

_____

_____

_____

_____

Support: _____

_____

_____

_____

_____

_____

Autonomy: _____

_____

_____

_____

Reinforcement: _____

_____

_____

_____

Organizing What You Know
About Key People

Use the following worksheets to record for each person, his or her

1. personal style;
2. relationship with you;
3. relationships with other key people;
4. pressures (job-related and other) to accept your ideas;
5. pressures (job-related and other) to resist your ideas.

❑ The Official Decision-Maker: _____

❑ The Opinion Leader: _____

❑ The Gatekeeper: _____

❑ The Consumer: _____

Personal Style: _____

_____

_____

Relationship with You: _____

_____

_____

Relationships with Other Key People: _____

_____

_____

Pressure to Accept Idea

Job-Related	Other

Pressure to Resist Idea

Job-Related	Other

Market Analysis of Key People

☐ The Official Decision-Maker: _____

☐ The Opinion Leader: _____

☐ The Gatekeeper: _____

☐ The Consumer: _____

Personal Style: _____

_____

_____

Relationship with You: _____

_____

_____

Relationships with Other Key People: _____

_____

_____

Pressure to Accept Idea

Job-Related	Other

Pressure to Resist Idea

Job-Related	Other

Market Analysis of Key People

☐ The Official Decision-Maker: _____

☐ The Opinion Leader: _____

☐ The Gatekeeper: _____

☐ The Consumer: _____

Personal Style: _____

_____

_____

Relationship with You: _____

_____

_____

Relationships with Other Key People: _____

_____

_____

Pressure to Accept Idea

Job-Related	Other

Pressure to Resist Idea

Job-Related	Other

Market Analysis of Key People

☐ The Official Decision-Maker: _____

☐ The Opinion Leader: _____

☐ The Gatekeeper: _____

☐ The Consumer: _____

Personal Style: _____

_____

_____

Relationship with You: _____

_____

_____

Relationships with Other Key People: _____

_____

_____

Pressure to Accept Idea

Job-Related	Other

Pressure to Resist Idea

Job-Related	Other

Writing a Win-Win Script

Using the following worksheets:

1. incorporate a person's strongest job-related reason to resist your idea into an empathy statement (statement of the other person's point of view);
2. select a connecting word (like "but" or "however") to tell your listener you're changing directions;
3. incorporate a person's strongest job-related reason to accept your idea in a statement of the problem as you see it;
4. select a connecting word (like "so" or "therefore") to tell your listener there's more to come;
5. accommodate major nonjob related pressures in the course of action you recommend.

Script

Key Person _____

Empathy Statement

_____

_____

_____

_____

Connecting Word

_____

Statement of Problem as You See It

_____

_____

_____

_____

_____

Connecting Word

_____

Conclusion (request, call for action, decision)

_____

_____

_____

_____

_____

_____

_____

Script

Key Person ————————————————————————————————

Empathy Statement

——

——

——

——

Connecting Word

——

Statement of Problem as You See It

——

——

——

——

Connecting Word

——

Conclusion (request, call for action, decision)

——

——

——

——

——

——

——

Script

Key Person _____

Empathy Statement

_____

_____

_____

_____

Connecting Word

_____

Statement of Problem as You See It

_____

_____

_____

_____

_____

Connecting Word

_____

Conclusion (request, call for action, decision)

_____

_____

_____

_____

_____

_____

_____

_____

Script

Key Person _____

Empathy Statement

_____

_____

_____

_____

Connecting Word

_____

Statement of Problem as You See It

_____

_____

_____

_____

_____

Connecting Word

_____

Conclusion (request, call for action, decision)

_____

_____

_____

_____

_____

_____

_____

_____

◆ Key II ◆

TAKE A CLOSER LOOK AT HOW PERSONAL STYLES WILL AFFECT PROJECT SUCCESS

The Case of Betty Ashford

Betty Ashford is also an engineer. Her project is another one with only loosely defined outcomes. The vice-president of science and engineering has (reluctantly) directed the development of a training program on cost controls in engineering. Betty is working with Roberta Houston, a training specialist, and with George Drexel, a finance specialist. Each team member is experienced in his own specialty but uninitiated in the other two. Furthermore, this is the first major project assignment for each of the three. (They consider the project major because of its high-level visibility even though no one is sure exactly how the output will be used.)

Because of the team's inexperience, Betty expected there to be no end to the squabbling within the team over whose way is the right way. But she was mistaken. There have been some problems within the team, all right. Betty found it especially hard to work with Roberta at first. Betty alternately felt crowded (as though Roberta just wouldn't leave her alone) and directionless (as though she just couldn't pin down Roberta's expectations). But with all three team members, getting the job done seemed to take precedence over individual differences. She felt the team was now really working as a team.

But dealing with top management was another matter. To begin with, there was Betty's own chain of command. Walter Pruitt, the engineering manager, isn't interfering. But he's not helping pave the way with top management for Betty, either. He just seems to want to be left out of it. And Edward Dalton, the vice-president of science and engineering, authorized the project only because of open criticism from Thomas Cartwright, vice-president of finance. Dalton is a low-keyed but powerful rival of Cartwright's. Like Cartwright, Dalton can be very persuasive. Unlike Cartwright, Dalton's loyalty is to the technology and to the mission not to the dollars. Dalton won't violate his principles, but you can expect him to oppose Cartwright whenever it's ethically possible.

The most difficult chain of command, however, has been George Drexel's. George's boss Thomas Cartwright has really been hard for Betty to take. Often called "Colonel," Cartwright's white hair, military bearing and booming, confident voice make a striking impression. He has the ability to sway people in his direction even when all previous decisions have gone the other way. He tends to present his ideas as rules or accepted facts. He's bright, thoroughly competent. But he's clearly interested only in dollars. He's not concerned about the environment or about the company's public image. Betty constantly feels crowded by Cartwright. It's not that he seems terribly controlling (although he does sometimes get a little pushy); it's just that he *always* seems to be right there. Betty feels she can't get away from him. And he seems almost flirtatious—hinting for compliments and demanding attention. In the following chapter, we'll see how Betty can take a closer look at how personal styles can affect project success. She can

- examine new roles and relationships;
- explore her own expectations and preferences;
- assess the amount of control she expects in general;
- study her behavior in specific relationships;
- choose the best course of action. Decide when to live and let live; when to modify her own behavior; when to give and get feedback about the effect a relationship is having on the job; when to negotiate for changes in behavior.

7

*T*aking a *C*loser *L*ook

INTRODUCTION

"An individual in his late 40s who worked for a large energy company was described to us by his former co-workers as 'a good geophysicist and a helluva lot of fun.' He was diagnosed by his physician as having terminal cancer. To the surprise of his co-workers, he continued to come into work each day until his death. When others remarked about it, he responded that, along with his home and family, this was where he had found satisfaction to this point in his life. He saw no reason to give up what he enjoyed." (Dalton & Thompson, 1986, 226)

"Three years ago, Jack was a computer company's research manager, content in his job and very ambitious. Top management offered him a promotion to a job as manager of administrative services. While at first Jack didn't like the position offered him, management persuaded him to accept it by arguing that it would be an important step in his career development. . . .

Jack has already spent three years in this job. . . . he spoke of the feeling of being trapped: 'I'm not really content in this job, but if I do well it will help me in my next job in research.

It's a thankless task, being at everybody's beck and call. The trouble is that it's getting to me. I can't take the strain much longer. I went to my boss last month and told him that I want to move back to research. He told me that they would take care of that in due time, that I was doing a grand job now, and that they needed me here" (Bartolomé and Evans, 1980, p. 142).

The fit between the geophysicist and his job was a good one that helped him endure personal tragedy with some sense of purpose. The fit between the former researcher and his job is a poor one that makes him miserable at work; and his misery is spilling over into his personal life as well.

A perfect fit occurs when three things happen at once: (1) A person feels competent in his job, (2) he enjoys his work, and (3) his moral values coincide with work values. When one of these three things is missing, a misfit occurs. (Bartolomé & Evans, 1980, p. 142).

When a technical specialist makes the shift to project manager, he may also shift from fitting to *mis*fitting. (1) He may not feel competent to get the work done through other people. (2) He may be unhappy away from the hands-on technical work. (3) He may find that the amount of time he must spend in meetings or dealing with individual problems conflicts with his work ethic to produce something.

The misfitting will adversely affect the job when the project manager copes by

- focusing too narrowly on the project itself without seeing broader organizational needs;
- locking himself inside
- failing to help others (Dalton & Thompson, 1986, pp. 75–85).

A project manager who knows himself well has a better chance of changing himself or changing the situation for a better fit. He should take a closer look at himself and the way he relates to other people. Specifically, he should take these steps:

Step A. *Examine new roles and relationships;*

Step B. *Assess the amount of control he expects in general;*

Step C. *Study his behavior in specific relationships: how he gives and gets inclusion, control, and affection;*

Step D. *Choose the best course of action.*

He can decide when to live and let live, when to modify his own behavior, when to give and get feedback about a relationship, and when to negotiate for a change in someone else's behavior. In this chapter we'll see how one project manager, Betty Ashford, uses what she learns about herself to make better decisions about relationships that affect her project.

◆ Step A ◆ EXAMINE NEW ROLES AND RELATIONSHIPS

Betty Ashford is an engineer. Her project has only loosely defined outcomes. The vice-president of science and engineering has (reluctantly) directed the development of a training program on cost controls in engineering. Betty is working with Roberta Houston, a training specialist, and with George Drexel, a finance specialist. Each team member is experienced in his own specialty but uninitiated in the other two. Furthermore, this is the first major project assignment for each of the three. (They consider the project major because of it's high-level visibility, even though no one is sure exactly how the output will be used.)

Betty's role as project manager will be different from her previous roles as team member. She'll get work done through other people now. Since she can't do it all herself, she'll need to develop abilities in others. Betty will set priorities instead of just accepting the ones she's given. And she'll need to market her project constantly, especially with her own top management.

In the first place, Betty must now get work done through other people. She may no longer choose to just go off to her own corner and grind the work out. Project managers who give in to the temptation to do that will find themselves (per Kepler's Law) going faster and faster in smaller and smaller circles like the project manager who said,

"We're barely making deadlines. We've managed to squeak by so far because I've done most of the work myself. I can't keep it up, I know. But when I try to get more work out of my people they either ask a lot of questions or mess things up or both. Either way, they waste a lot of my time and I wind up doing it myself anyway."

To avert Kepler's Law, Betty stays in frequent two-way communication about goals, about work standards, about deadlines. But she is constantly aware of her natural inclination to do it all herself.

Her need to get the work done without doing it all herself requires Betty to accept responsibility for developing her team members. On this project no team member has experience in another's area of expertise, so she needs some cross-training as well. It's not necessary for each team member to become expert in each field, but each needs to be at least literate in the other specialties involved. In several instances, she has said to herself, "Roberta can't do that, so I'll just do it myself!" But that road leads back to Kepler's Law. And it cheats Roberta of the learning value of this assignment as well.

As a team member, Betty has accepted priorities as assigned. As project manager, she must help set, assess, and monitor priorities. It wouldn't be enough to decide where the rivets on the bridge should be placed; Betty must help decide whether the bridge should be built at all.

However she sets priorities, they will be constantly competing with other priorities for the attention of her team, of her client, and of her top management. So Betty must be constantly marketing her project. In fact, Betty's most difficult selling job could be to her own line management: a supervisor who wants to be left out of it and a vice-president who authorized the project reluctantly.

This public relations role is a major shift from her role as technical specialist. And it can be a major drain on Betty's energy and morale. If she were not prepared for this role, she could wind up like the scientist who said,

"It's the 'salesmen' and papershufflers who get the high ratings around here, not the scientists. I'm not saying a lot of them aren't good scientists, but you have to leave science if you want to have a future around here. In fact, a career in science doesn't seem much like I thought it would be. I know my field; I publish; I'm a better scientist than a lot of those guys who seem to be 'fairhaired boys,' but I don't see anything to look forward to. I didn't go into science for the money; that isn't it. I just can't see any future, and that's no way to live" (Dalton and Thompson, 1986, p. 80).

The need to sell a project will make more routine contact with top management and with the client necessary. In Betty's project top management is her client. So any awkward relationship seems doubly so. George Drexel's boss Thomas Cartwright has really been difficult to take. He tends to present his ideas as rules or accepted facts—even when all previous decisions have gone the other way. And Betty constantly feels crowded by him. It's not that he seems terribly controlling (although he does sometimes get a little pushy); but he always seems to be right there. Betty feels she can't seem to get away from him. And he seems almost flirtatious—hinting for compliments and demanding attention.

◆ Step B ◆ ASSESS THE AMOUNT OF CONTROL YOU EXPECT IN GENERAL

Traditionally, management has recruited people for its own ranks who believe that they themselves have control of events. (The research literature refers to these as people with a strong internal orientation.) But project management is different. People often don't really have control. And they are more likely to succeed when they recognize their limits (have an external orientation). One study (Dailey, 1978, pp. 311–316) found that project leaders with an external orientation

- had happier team members;
- had higher performing teams. In fact, the more external the orientation of the leader, the higher team performance. This relationship is the strongest as task uncertainty increases.

One measure of internal-external orientation is the Rotter Scale (Rotter, 80, pp. 1–28). Let's look at the scores of two team members on selected items. Betty's responses are in Figure 7-1.

Betty's scores on these items—as on the scale as a whole—show a strong internal orientation. Not surprising for someone with her technical background. Betty may find it difficult to release some of the work into the hands of her team members. And she may find it frustrating to deal with the management decisions beyond her control.

Roberta's responses are in Figure 7-2. Her scores on these items—as well as her response to the scale as a whole—show a mixed orientation. She would have less difficulty dealing with the things

Figure 7–1
Betty's Responses to Selected Items on the Rotter Scale

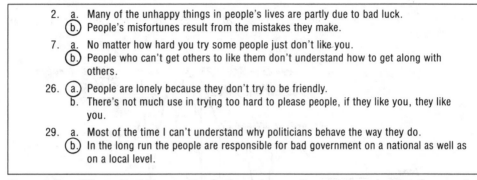

> 2.   a. Many of the unhappy things in people's lives are partly due to bad luck.
>   (b.) People's misfortunes result from the mistakes they make.
> 7.   a. No matter how hard you try some people just don't like you.
>   (b.) People who can't get others to like them don't understand how to get along with others.
> 26. (a.) People are lonely because they don't try to be friendly.
>   b. There's not much use in trying too hard to please people, if they like you, they like you.
> 29. a. Most of the time I can't understand why politicians behave the way they do.
>   (b.) In the long run the people are responsible for bad government on a national as well as on a local level.

Rotter, Julian. "Generalized Expectancies for Internal versus External Control of Reinforcement,"
Psychological Monographs: General and Applied. *80(1), 1966, 1–28. Copyright 1966 by the*
American Psychological Association. Reprinted by permission of the publisher and the author.

Figure 7–2
Roberta's Responses to Selected Items on the Rotter Scale

> 2.   (a.) Many of the unhappy things in people's lives are partly due to bad luck.
>   b. People's misfortunes result from the mistakes they make.
> 7.   a. No matter how hard you try some people just don't like you.
>   (b.) People who can't get others to like them don't understand how to get along with others.
> 26. a. People are lonely because they don't try to be friendly.
>   (b.) There's not much use in trying too hard to please people, if they like you, they like you.
> 29. a. Most of the time I can't understand why politicians behave the way they do.
>   (b.) In the long run the people are responsible for bad government on a national as well as on a local level.

Rotter, Julian. "Generalized Expectancies for Internal versus External Control of Reinforcement,"
Psychological Monographs: General and Applied. *80(1), 1966, 1–28. Copyright 1966 by the*
American Psychological Association. Reprinted by permission of the publisher and the author.

beyond her control than Betty. On the other hand, she could be less at ease with line management responsibilities.

Betty can also use a less scientific, but very revealing, technique to assess her outlook on control (and other dimensions of the job): a lifeline. Guided strictly by her feelings (not structured by logical criteria), Betty graphed the highs and lows in her life and labelled the life events that went with them.

Figure 7–3
First Drawing of Betty's Lifeline

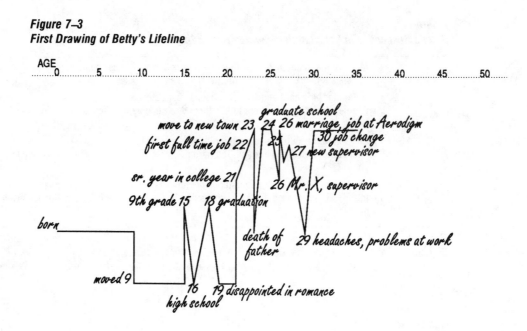

Before we see how Betty analyzed her lifeline, draw your own (without logical criteria) here.

Figure 7–4
Your Own Lifeline

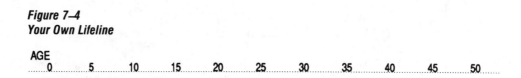

Then she reviewed her graph and identified characteristics of the work-related highs and lows.

Figure 7–5
Analysis of Betty's Lifeline

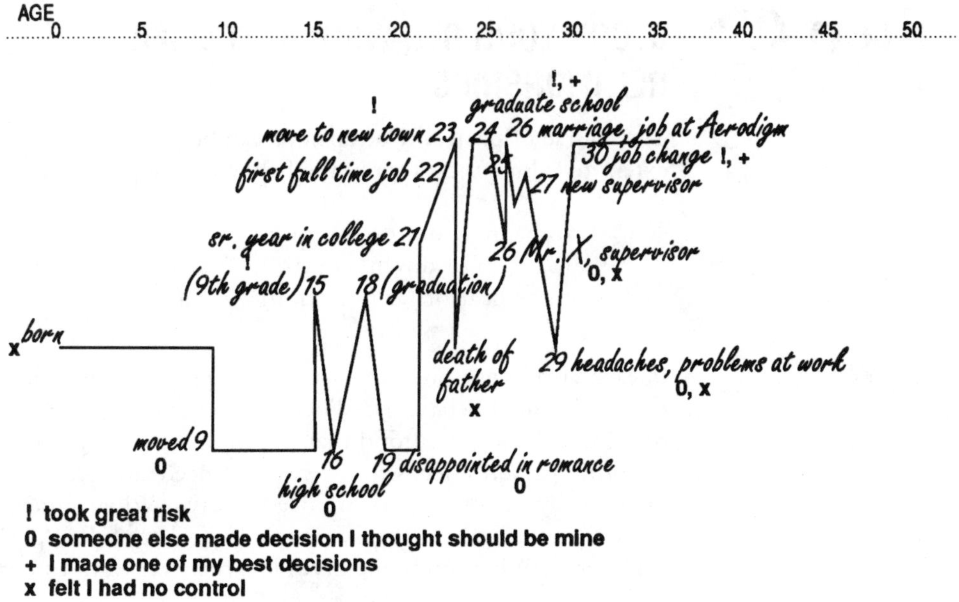

! took great risk
0 someone else made decision I thought should be mine
+ I made one of my best decisions
x felt I had no control

She found that the work-related highs were consistently characterized by

- risk-taking;
- sense of control;
- freedom to make decisions that were important to her;
- hands-on work.

The work-related lows were consistently characterized by

- routine;
- lack of control over elements of the job;
- decisions she thought should be her own made by someone else;
- process work that seems to have no actual product.

Now you can go back to Figure 7-4 and analyze your work-related highs and lows by these or other criteria.

Both the Rotter Scale and the lifeline have helped Betty identify elements of her personal style that may be roadblocks in this project. But a good working knowledge of herself can prepare Betty to work through or go around the blocks.

◆ Step C ◆ STUDY YOUR BEHAVIOR IN SPECIFIC RELATIONSHIPS

The course of project relationships can be greatly affected by the extent to which they supply the behaviors each person wants

- to be in or out (inclusion);
- to be up or down (control);
- to be near or far (affection).

In each area, a person wants to give (expressed behavior) and receive (wanted behavior). When we feel that a relationship is just right, the chances are good that our needs to give are matched by the other person's needs to receive; our needs to receive are matched by the other person's need to give. When someone gives more than we want to receive, we may feel crowded, pushed, or smothered. When someone gives less than we want to receive we may feel left out, impotent, or rejected.

A scale to measure these preferences in a relationship grew out of efforts at the Naval Research Laboratory to improve the performance of a CIC (Combat Information Center). The Fundamental Interpersonal Relationship Orientation Survey (FIRO-B) can help a person identify his preferences in a relationship and talk about them without blaming, attacking, or retreating. It can help alert a person to opportunities in a relationship to reinforce the things that go well and to make in-flight corrections of those things that don't. The scale can be administered only by someone licensed to do so. The scale and licensing information are available through Consulting Psychologist Press, Palo Alto, CA.

A person could benefit most from the scale by actually taking it, of course. And we will add scores of key people to our discussion here. But Betty could learn a lot about her relationships by just thinking through the major concepts.

If a person feels crowded, then other people may want to include him more than he wants to be included. He may feel he doesn't have the chance to be alone as much as he would like. Betty and Roberta are both likely to feel crowded in their relationship.

Figure 7–6
Inclusion Scores for Betty and for Roberta

Compare the expressed inclusion of Betty with the wanted inclusion of Roberta (shaded squares). Then compare the expressed inclusion of Roberta with the wanted inclusion of Betty (clear squares). Both team members are likely to feel crowded.

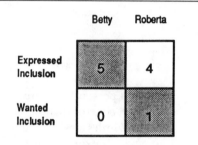

If a person feels left out, then he may want other people to include him more than they do. Cartwright is likely to feel this way in a relationship with Roberta.

Figure 7–7
Inclusion Scores for Betty and for Cartwright

Compare the expressed inclusion of Betty with the wanted inclusion of Cartwright (shaded squares). Cartwright could feel left out.

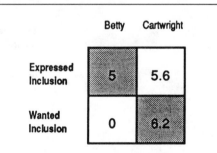

If a person feels pushed, then other people may want to control him more than he wants to be controlled. He may feel other people too often or too forcefully tell him what to do. Roberta may feel this way in her relationship with Betty.

Figure 7–8
Control Sources for Betty and for Roberta

Compare the expressed control of Betty to the wanted control of Roberta (shaded squares). Roberta may feel pushed.

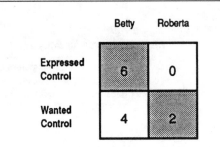

If a person feels directionless, the other people may want to give less control than he wants to receive. He may feel a certain amount of aimlessness in the relationship. Or he may feel confused about what's expected of him. Betty might feel this way in her relationship with Roberta.

Figure 7–9
Control Sources for Betty and for Roberta, a Second Look

Compare the expressed control of Roberta with the wanted control of Betty (clear squares). Betty may feel directionless in trying to relate to Roberta.

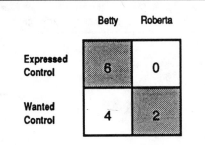

If a person feels smothered, then other people may want to be closer than he wants them to be or give more affection than he wants. People don't often get more affection than they want. No one in this case study does. (Cartwright isn't giving Betty more than she wants, he's wanting more than she gives.) But here's a hypothetical set of scores to illustrate.

Figure 7–10
Affection Scores for Two Imaginary People

No one on Betty's team is getting more affection than he or she wants. (Not many people off Betty's team are, either!) But compare the expressed affection of imaginary Person A with the wanted affection of the imaginary Person B (shaded squares). Person B could feel smothered.

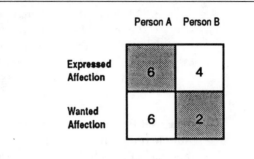

If a person feels rejected, then other people may want less closeness than he does or want to give less affection (at work—approval or recognition) than he wants to receive. He may feel the other person is cool or unfriendly toward him. Both Cartwright and Roberta are likely to feel this way in the relationship with Betty.

Figure 7–11
Affection Scores for Betty with Roberta and with Cartwright

Compare the expressed affection of Betty with the wanted affection of both Roberta and Cartwright (shaded squares). Both Roberta and Cartwright could feel rejected by Betty.

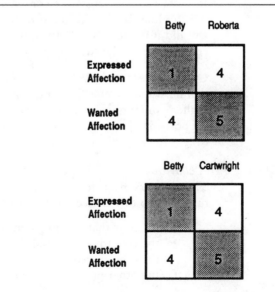

✦ Step D ✦   CHOOSE THE BEST COURSE OF ACTION

When something in a relationship doesn't fit, a person is faced with these basic choices.

- Just allow for the differences. Live and let live.
- Modify his own behavior.
- Give and get feedback about how the preferences are affecting the relationship (or the job).
- Negotiate an agreement for a change in his own behavior and in the other person's.

Live and let live

The usefulness of this approach is decided by the answer to one simple question: "Does it matter?" If the answer is "no," then this approach can help lighten the load in a relationship. If the answer is "yes," then this approach can only add to the burden the relationship must bear.

At first Betty found Roberta especially difficult to deal with. It seemed that Roberta's every opinion was ambivalent: "I think we should. . . . Well, what I really mean is. . . ." Betty felt like pleading, "Will you *please* make up your mind!' She wanted Roberta to be more forceful, more directive. But after Betty got a handle on her own impatience and *really* listened, she better understood what was happening. Roberta used a few qualifying statements habitually—just as some people use "well" or "uh." Her style was to be uncontrolling, nondirective. But the substance of Roberta's suggestions were consistent—and consistently worthwhile. Betty still found Roberta's habitual phrases annoying. But did it matter? No. Betty just chose to ignore them and concentrate on the substance instead.

On the other hand, Walter Pruitt has said from the very beginning that he wanted to be "left out of it." Betty's uneasiness with Walter's uninvolvement grows. Does it matter? Yes. Walter's support may be critical to her project's success. Betty won't be able to ignore the problem.

Modify his own behavior

The one person's behavior a project manager can surely control is his own. So this choice can be a useful one whenever

- it's clear that it is his own behavior that is out of line;
- the cost to him of making a change is minimal, the cost to the other person great;
- the other person is unable to change.

Betty has often felt that other people crowded her. Now she sees that it could hardly be any other way: her "Wanted Inclusion" score was zero. When other team members have asked her to join them for lunch, Betty has always replied, "Sorry, I have plans," and then eaten the lunch she brought from home alone in her office. Now she sees that she's indulging an extreme preference that can block her team building. Next time she'll say "Sure!"

George really pressed to get a computerized report for the group by June 27. Unfortunately, he had misread Betty's note about the format she wanted. True, the format she requested would have been easier to follow, but she can still interpret the data accurately. And her reputation won't be affected. On the other hand, if George made a change now, he would lose face with Cartwright and really be hassled by his computer staff. These are all people he works with daily—people whose respect he wants. Those aren't necessary costs for him to bear right now. Betty can adjust to the format until it's time for the next report.

Betty used to give her old secretary information on the run, as she dashed through the outer office, and had no problems. But the new secretary seemed to be ignoring her. Betty felt rejected by her new employee. Then a co-worker told Betty about the new secretary's hearing problem. Now Betty stops at the secretary's desk and makes eye contact before she speaks.

Give and get feedback about how the preferences are affecting the relationship (or the job)

Sometimes it's clear that something about a relationship is getting in the way. It's clear that it matters. It's not clear what to do about it. Then it's time simply to talk about it without anger in nonjudgmental terms.

Roberta, for example, simply got lost during some of the technical discussions between Betty and George. At first she just felt ignorant and unwanted; she simply withdrew. But she realized she couldn't make much of a contribution if she didn't know what was going on. Finally, she mustered up her courage and said, "I feel like a dummy when you get into one of those technical discussions. How can I get caught up without slowing you two down?"

Negotiate for a change in the other person's behavior (perhaps accompanied by a change in his own)

Sometimes it's important, a change in the project manager's behavior alone would harm the project, and at least part of the solution is clear. Then it's time for the project manager to ask for what he wants.

Walter Pruitt's support of Betty's project is important. If Betty simply changes her behavior by agreeing to leave Walter out of it her project will suffer. Part of the solution is clearly Walter's participation in project updates. It's time for Betty to ask him to participate.

SUMMARY

A project is more likely to succeed when there is a good fit between the project manager and the job itself and a good fit between the project manager and other key people. To engineer the best fit a project manager should take a closer look at himself by following these steps.

Step A. Examine new roles and relationships

What will be the impact of new role functions: To get the job done through other people? To develop team members? To set, assess, and monitor priorities? To market his project? To maintain routine contact with top management and with the client?

Step B. Assess the amount of control he expects in general

An external orientation varies positively with team satisfaction and with team productivity. Both the Rotter Scale and a less formal technique—the lifeline—can help a project manager look more closely at his expectation of control.

Step C. Study his behavior in specific relationships

Project relationships will be greatly affected by the extent to which they satisfy a person's wishes for inclusion, for control, and for affection.

Step D. Choose the best course of action

He can
- Live and let live when the differences really don't matter.
- Modify his own behavior when his own behavior is out of line, when he could minimize individual costs, or when the other person cannot change.
- Give and get feedback when the difference matters but the solution isn't clear.
- Negotiate for a change in the other person's behavior when the difference matters, when a change by the project manager alone would harm the project, and when at least part of the solution is clear.

Examining New Roles and Relationships

Ask yourself these questions about how the project manager's role will affect relationships.

1. How will relationships be affected by your new role to get work done through other people? What signals do you see that you are falling under Kepler's Law?
   - Are you pulling back decision-making authority that you have delegated?
     —Are you overinvolving yourself in work you have already delegated?
     —Are you focusing more and more intensely on procedures of greater and greater detail?
   - Does success seem more dependent on sheer endurance or brute strength than on skill or knowledge?

2. How will relationships be affected by your responsibility to develop team members?
   - Can you recognize development needs without feeling angry about them?
   - Will you take the time to develop your people instead of doing it all yourself?
   - Are you willing to let some people be better than others at some things, not as good as others at some things?

3. How will relationships be affected by your responsibility to set and track priorities?
   - Are you thinking about *whether* something should be done or just *how* it should be done?
   - Are you getting input about priorities from other team members? From your client? From management?
   - Are you following up without overcontrolling?

4. How will relationships be affected by your need to market your project?
   - Are you resisting this responsibility? (Do you feel you're being dragged into office politics against your will?)
   - Are you feeling angry toward people who aren't sold? Are you shutting them out?

5. How will relationships be affected by your need for routine contact with higher management and with your client?
- Is it awkward for you to deal face-to-face with people at different levels?
- Are you being overcritical?
- Are you stifling your opinions?

Assessing Control In General

If possible, respond to the Rotter Scale. (Rotter, n. d., (1), 1–28.) If you did not complete this activity as you read the text of Chapter Seven, graph the highs and lows in your life on the chart below. Label them with life events.

Your Own Lifeline

AGE
0 .... 5 .... 10 .... 15 .... 20 .... 25 .... 30 .... 35 .... 40 .... 45 .... 50 ....

Now go back and analyze the work related highs and lows. You can code them this way:

! I took a great risk.
* I played it safe.
0 Someone else made a major decision I thought should be mine.
+ I made one of my best decisions.
× I felt I had no control.
I was in control.

List the characteristics of the highs:

-

-

-

-

-

List the characteristics of the lows:

-

-

-

-

-

Studying Your Behavior

If possible, respond to the FIRO-B. (Available to certified professionals through Consulting Psychologists Press, Palo Alto, CA.)

Answer these questions about your relationships with other key people.

1. Around which people do you feel crowded? These people may want to include you more than you want to be included.

_____

_____

2. Around which people do you feel left out? You may want to be included more than these people want to include you.

_____

_____

3. Around which people do you feel pushed? These people may want to control you more than you want them to.

_____

_____

4. Around which people do you feel directionless? You may want these people to exert more control than they want.

_____

_____

5. Around which people do you feel smothered? These people may want to give you more affection than you want to receive.

_____

_____

6. Around which people do you feel rejected? These people may give you less affection than you want.

_____

_____

Choosing the Best Course of Action

Your answers to these questions can help you choose.

1. Does the difference between what you want and what you're getting matter? _____. If it doesn't, just live and let live.

2. Is it clear that your own behavior is out of line? _____.
   Is the cost of changing your behavior small while the cost to the other person of changing his behavior is great? _____.
   Is the other person unable to change? _____.

   If the answer to these questions is yes, consider modifying your own behavior.

3. Is it clear that something about a relationship is getting in the way but not clear what to do about it? _____.
   If you answered yes then give and get feedback about how behavior preferences are affecting the relationship or the project.

4. Does the behavior matter? _____. Would a change in your behavior alone harm the project? _____. Is at least part of the solution clear? _____.

   If you answered yes to all three questions then negotiate for a change in the other person's behavior.

◆ Key III ◆

HANDLE THE CONFLICT

The Case of Carl White

Carl White, engineer, has a project with well-defined outcomes. In addition, his project team is quite experienced in the project technology. He expected his biggest problem to be developing teamwork within his group. And he was right.

Carl's assignment is to work with one person from each branch of science and engineering to revise operations standards. Personality clashes have made progress slow from the very beginning. Carl suspects that several alleged technical disputes have been thinly veiled personality issues as well.

Carl has had a hard time getting through a commitment to priorities so that work can be scheduled and staffing decisions (along with other administrative decisions) can be made. Fred Kemp, the team member from maintenance, can't seem to decide if he's in the group or out. Brad Thornton from production doesn't seem to want any responsibility himself. But he appears to be doing his best to block Carl's leadership. Enid Schwartz from methods and standards actually appears to be supportive—but she is somewhat withdrawn. Jack Thompson, from quality assurance, is used to being in charge. He obviously thinks he would be a more capable, more efficient project leader than Carl.

The success of Carl's project will depend largely on his ability to handle the conflict within his team. In the following chapters, we'll see how he can:

- expect the conflict and plan how to handle it (Chapter Eight);
- have his own stress management techniques in place before the project begins (Chapter Eight);
- serve as a lightning rod: listen and reflect (Chapter Nine);
- excavate the real issues underlying a conflict (Chapter Nine);
- look for win-win alternatives (Chapter Ten);
- cut his losses when necessary (Chapter Ten).

8

Preparing for the Conflict

INTRODUCTION

Project management solves one dilemma: how to get maximum technical and professional input across specialties. But it creates another: it changes the worry curve. Instead of doing all the worry during the last 10 percent of the project (when it may be too late), people worry from the very beginning. The worry and the need to cross organizational boundaries make conflict inherent.

And project management is subject to The Fatal Law of Gravity: When you are down, everything falls on you. So the project manager's success, in large part, will depend on his ability to manage in an environment with many "downers" without getting down himself. This six-step strategy can help.

Step A.   *Expect conflict and plan ahead how to handle it.*
Step B.   *Have your own stress management techniques in place before the project begins.*
Step C.   *Be a lightning rod.*
Step D.   *Excavate the issues.*
Step E.   *Look for win-win alternatives.*
Step F.   *Cut your losses when necessary.*

In this chapter we'll develop the first two steps—the two a project manager must have in place to be prepared for conflict when it comes. In the next chapters we'll develop the remaining four steps—the four a project manager can use in the heat of a given conflict.

And we'll see how project manager Carl White uses these steps to handle the conflict within his team.

◆ Step A ◆   EXPECT CONFLICT AND PLAN AHEAD HOW TO HANDLE IT

Expect conflict

What exactly should a project manager expect? For one thing, he can expect sources of conflict to vary with phases of a project's life cycle:

- Project Formulation Phase (from the conception of the project to the commitment of funds and staff);
- Build-up Phase (from the assignment of the first person to full staffing);
- Main Program Phase (from full staffing to the completion of primary objectives);
- Phase-out (from the completion of primary objectives to the reassignment of the last person).

To see how your expectations about conflict compare with those of about 100 other project managers, respond to this questionnaire. There are no right or wrong answers, just *opinions*. So just quickly jot down your instinctive reactions.

Conflict Questionnaire

1. Put a numeral *1* by the item you'd expect to be the most intense source of conflict during the project formulation phase. Put a *2*

by the second most intense source, a *3* by the third most intense, and so on until every item is numbered.

2. Which of the seven sources of conflict listed did project managers feel was usually the most difficult to resolve?

3. Which did they say was most persistent over time?

Table 8–1
Seven Sources of Conflict to Rank

	Project Formulation	Build-Up	Main Program	Phase-Out
Schedules				
Priorities				
Manpower				
Technical Issues				
Administration				
Personality				
Cost				

Blake and Mouton (1964) identify five styles of handling conflict.

- Withdrawal
- Smoothing—De-emphasizing disagreement and emphasizing agreement
- Compromising
- Forcing—Imposing one's view on others; this usually results in a win-lose situation.
- Confrontation—Facing conflict directly and using a problem solving approach. (Note that the Blake and Mouton definition is different from the usual connotation of "confrontation." Their definition more closely matches the current use of the term "assertiveness.")

4. Which style did project managers favor overall?

5. Which was their second choice?

6. Which did project managers prefer to use in dealing with higher management?

7. Which did they prefer to use in dealing with peers?

8. Which was the least favored style of project managers?

Now compare your answers with those of about 100 other project managers in a survey by Thaimhain and Wilemon (1975, pp. 31–50).

1. Table 8-2 shows how project managers ranked the source of conflict.

Sources of conflict for the project overall received these rankings:

Schedules	1
Priorities	2
Manpower	3
Technical Issues	4
Administration	5
Personality	6
Cost	7

Table 8–2
Survey Rankings of Seven Sources of Conflict

	Project Formulation	Build-Up	Main Program	Phase-Out
Schedules	3	2	1	1
Priorities	1	1	4	4
Manpower	4	5	3	3
Technical Issues	6	4	2	6
Administration	2	3	5	7
Personality	7	6	7	2
Cost	5	7	6	5

2. Which of the seven sources of conflict listed did project managers feel was usually the most difficult to resolve?

   Personality

3. Which did they say was most persistent over time?

   Personality

4. Which style did project managers favor overall?

Confrontation

5. Which was their second choice?

Compromising

6. Which did project managers prefer to use in dealing with higher management?

Confrontation

7. Which did they prefer to use in dealing with peers?
Compromising

8. Which was the least favored style of project managers?

Withdrawal

Some people are surprised by the relatively low overall rank of cost. At least one project manager thinks it *ought* to get a higher ranking. He thinks many project "champions" underestimate startup costs and then shortchange reasonable expenses, fast-track the schedule, and compromise technical standards (Gilbreath, 1986, p. 37). However, others have found that cost is *not* a major variable in determining project success (Baker and others, 1983, p. 670).

And some feel that the low overall ranking of personality contradicts the response that personality was the most difficult source of conflict to resolve and the most persistent over time. Project managers respond that although they would never rank personality as the number one source at any time, it is consistently one of the most frustrating sources to deal with. And they further suspect that personality conflicts are often disguised as technical or other issues. They often *suspect* a disguise, but it's hard to be sure.

The high rank of schedules as a source of conflict doesn't surprise anyone. Hyrum Smith, a time management consultant, tells of asking a group of executives "Why haven't you read all those good books on your 'To Do' List?" One war-weary executive quickly replied, "Books don't ring" (Smith, 1986, Tape I). They don't storm angrily into a manager's office, either. And interruptions by phone and by visit are just two of the many attackers on scheduling.

At first glance it seems a little startling that project managers are willing to compromise with their peers but more likely to confront higher management. On the other hand, perhaps it is more important to have "every 'i' dotted and every 't' crossed" when dealing with the people who have the most control over us.

Conflict sources and their intensity will vary across the life cycle of a project. And we can expect the focus of conflict to vary with the attributes of the project as well.

Table 8–3
Attributes of a Project and Focus of Conflict

	Extent of Agreement on Outcomes	
Experience with Technology	Loosely-defined Outcomes	Well-defined Outcomes
High Company Experience	Conflict within Team and Conflict between Team and the Outside Equally High	Higher Conflict within Team
Low Company Experience	Higher Conflict between Team and the Outside	Both Equally Low

Where does Carl White's project fall? Carl's assignment is to work with one person from each branch of science and engineering to revise operations standards. On the surface, the conflicts Carl is facing are those he expected in the build-up phase of a project.

- Establishing priorities seems to be the biggest problem. Carl just can't seem to get his team members to agree on what's important and what isn't.

- Scheduling is held at bay while the team debates priorities. Team members seem eager to make schedule commitments for pet objectives. But unless they can agree on priorities, there will actually be three or four individual subprojects underway, not one team effort.
- Administrative issues are another active source of contention. Who shares information with whom, who reports to whom, who makes which decisions—these issues are the subject of seemingly endless debate.

Carl's project has well-defined outcomes in the eyes of top management. And his project team is an experienced one. He expected his biggest problem to be developing teamwork within the group and he was right. In fact, Carl suspects that personality conflict has been the culprit from the very beginning. There certainly are valid issues about priorities, about schedules, about administration. But Carl believes that these valid issues are often only the thin disguises of a personality clash.

Plan ahead how to deal with it

Carl had realistic expectations about conflict within his team. But how can he plan to deal with it? He can

- develop a mental framework that allows him to view conflict nonjudgmentally;
- analyze key people in his market;
- write a tentative script with which to approach each key person.

Develop a mental framework that allows him to view conflict nonjudgmentally

William Schutz (1958, 123–135) says that conflict in groups comes from the struggle of each person to answer these questions about his role: Am I in or out? Am I up or down? Am I near or far?

Am I in or out? Do I belong to this group or not? These questions are often the first source of conflict in a group. People dealing with this conflict are likely to raise issues unimportant in themselves just to test the water. Just as people talk about the weather because they want some harmless way to size another person up—not because they *really* care about the weather. If an issue sounds like something you would discuss at a cocktail party, it probably falls into this category. Schutz refers to such issues as "goblet issues." Fred Kemp, the member of Carl's team from maintenance, still seems to be asking whether he's a member of the group or not.

Fred realizes he gives the appearance of wavering in and out of the team. But he just doesn't have the confidence he needs to fully participate in the project. Maintenance and production are often allies on issues within the company so he would like to give Brad Thornton's point of view support whenever possible. But Brad is such a disagreeable sort it's hard to separate his real point of view from his potshots. So Fred finds himself resenting Brad more and more and withdrawing more and more from team participation. Fred's boss doesn't really support Fred's participation in this project, either. In fact, when he knows Fred is due at a team meeting, he applies pressure on Fred to do something else. Carl has seen several indicators that Fred is stuck at this initial question: Fred alternates between talking too much and withdrawing completely; when he does talk he seems intent on sharing his life story; and he interrupts a train of thought to tell his own war stories.

Am I up or down? Those who decide they are in will then be interested in authority issues. Are they at the top or at the bottom? How will the group make decisions? How much responsibility, how much influence, how much control will each person have? Carl's group as a whole is now dealing with this question. Two members seem to have a special investment in it. Brad Thornton from production doesn't seem to want any responsibility himself. But he appears to be doing his best to block Carl's leadership. To Carl's every comment, Brad tags on "But that's not really the point," or "That would never work." Brad seems much more interested in complaining than in solving any problems. On the other hand, Jack Thompson from quality assurance seems to want full responsibility and control. He shares some constructive ideas. But he almost always introduces them with "Wouldn't it be a better idea to . . ," or "I would handle it this way. . . ."

Am I near or far? Questions about openness and affection surface here. Like courting porcupines, team members must decide how they can get close enough to stay warm without getting stuck or hurt. Heightened emotions at this stage may express themselves positively or negatively: openly expressed positive feelings and warmth or open hostility and jealousy. Enid Schwartz, Carl's team member from methods and standards, is approaching this stage. She seems to give support to Fred and other team members in a low-keyed but steady way. She even manages to give that same steady support to her own supervisor, Chris Latham. She seems mildly amused by Lathams' arrogance—but not put off by it. She can hold her own in a disagreement and generally does so without raising defenses.

Carl uses these three questions—In or out? Up or down? Near or far?—as a nonjudgmental framework. When Fred launches into yet another war story, Carl can say to himself, "Fred is still asking 'In or out?'" When Jack interrupts with one more "Wouldn't it be a better idea . . .," Carl can say to himself "Jack is still asking 'Up or down?'" Carl doesn't have to escalate an issue unintentionally by judging or raising defenses.

Analyze key people in his "market"

Carl did a market analysis for the project as a whole before the project began. But he'll need to analyze some individual situations as well. How, for example, will he prepare to talk to Brad about Brad's demoralizing comments in project meetings? Figure 8-1 shows Carl's market analysis.

Write a tentative "script" to approach each key person

In this instance Brad's strongest job-related reason to resist Carl's plan is pressure from Mark Johnson. Marks wants him to undermine the project as a whole. Carl will use this reason to resist as the main idea in his empathy statement to Brad.

Brad's strongest job-related reason to go along with Carl is his wish to be seen as a capable person—not the person who caused a project to fail. Carl will include this reason in his statement of the problem.

Brad has a couple of non job-related pressures which Carl may not approach directly. But he will try to accommodate them in the course of action he proposes.

Figure 8-2 shows Carl's script.

◆ Step B ◆ HAVE YOUR OWN STRESS MANAGEMENT TECHNIQUES IN PLACE BEFORE THE PROJECT BEGINS

"I don't mind your hard work. I don't mind your long hours. But I do mind your being in a fog when you're supposed to be at home. Your body may be sitting in the den, but your brain's back at the office. Sometimes I think you leave your heart and soul there, too!"

Figure 8–1
Carl's Market Analysis of Brad

☒ The Official Decision-Maker: *Brad Thornton* _____
(For this situation)
☐ The Opinion Leader: _____

☐ The Gatekeeper: _____

☐ The Consumer: _____

Personal Style: *Capable. But surly and sarcastic. Seems more interested in complaining than in problem solving.*

Relationship with You: *Not much contact. I have said "Good morning" to Brad in hallway. He walked on without acknowledging.*

Relationships with Other Key People: *Other relationships don't seem any better. Possible exception is Enid Schwartz. Brad doesn't make negative remarks after Enid's input. Did I even see him nod in agreement once?*

Pressure to Accept Idea

Job-Related	Other
* Brad is capable. Probably doesn't want to be seen as contributor to failure.	** If he believes his behavior looks uncooperative he may have some need to maintain esteem with Enid.*

Pressure to Resist Idea

Job-Related	Other
* Brad's boss Mark Johnson will put pressure on Brad to undermine the idea of standards. ** Brad may actually believe common sense works better than formal standards anyway.* ** Brad doesn't have confidence in team products.*	** Seems to be contentious by nature.* ** May use negativism to build himself up in Enid's eyes.*

Figure 8–2
Carl's Script for Conversation with Brad

Key Person *Brad Thornton*

Empathy Statement

Brad, I realize Mark doesn't think revised operating standards are worth the effort. And maybe you think common sense is a better guide yourself. Besides, it's hard to be sure what kind of result you'll get from a group effort. Sometimes there are so many compromises nobody is satisfied.

Connecting Word

But...

Statement of Problem as You See It

...all eyes are on us now. Ed Dalton has given this project high priority. And Bedford Haynes is keeping a watchful eye on it. We would each be hurt by a high visibility project that floundered. And I'm afraid we will flounder if we don't get these control issues settled and get on with it.

Connecting Word

So...

Conclusion (request, call for action, decision)

I'd like for you to help in one of two ways:

1. When you believe an idea won't work, please just jot your objections down and talk to me about them individually right after the team meeting. If there's a problem you and I can't work out, then we can bring it up with the team.

Or

2. If you foresee a problem at the upcoming team meeting, maybe you and Enid could discuss it first. She could probably help generate some solutions to present to the group.

Carl hadn't realized he was taking his work home with him. And he wasn't taking the papers—just the problems. Until his wife pointed it out to him rather sharply, he hadn't noticed his apparent indifference, his fatigue, his crankiness. His wife gets credit for Carl's taking the first of two important steps in stress management:

- recognize a stressful situation in time to do something about it;
- tell yourself you can handle the stressful situation calmly.

Recognize a stressful situation in time to do something about it

In 1873 Samuel Plimsoll published *Our Seamen,* an attack on owners of unseaworthy, overloaded "coffin ships." Plimsoll claimed owners knowingly risked the heavily insured crafts and the lives of crewmen by loading ships to an unsafe depth. His outcry eventually led to the Merchant Shipping Act of 1875 which required the inscription of a load line on every ship. This Plimsoll line showed the depth to which the ship could be safely loaded without imminent risk of going under.

We, too, can be so heavily loaded that we are in imminent risk of going under. Unfortunately, no Plimsoll line warns us or those around us that we have all we can safely handle. We have to draw the line ourselves. If we pay attention, our bodies will tell us where our personal Plimsoll lines belong.

Carl hadn't been paying attention. He had ignored the queasy feeling in his stomach, the new difficulty falling asleep, the withdrawal at home. Not until his wife pointed out the problem did Carl make the connection: his work had loaded him with stress to an unsafe level.

Enid's body will signal in other ways that she has reached her personal Plimsoll line. She'll have a tight feeling in her chest and an uncomfortably dry mouth.

What signals does your body give? Unless you have a health reason not to try it, spend a minute or so with your eyes closed. Picture yourself at an upcoming meeting that you dread. Does the muscle at the back of your neck tighten? Do your hands feel clammy? Do you feel faint?

Whatever signal your body gives, pay attention to it. And the next time you get that signal, recognize it as a warning that you're approaching your personal Plimsoll line: you are in stress.

Tell yourself you can handle the stressful situation calmly

Once Carl noticed his Plimsoll line, he started unloading some stresses and increasing his capacity to handle others. These were some of his tactics:

- He gave himself mental encouragement.
- He looked for the humor in the situation.
- He found ways to work smarter instead of harder.
- He practiced deep breathing and muscle relaxation exercises.
- He asserted himself.

Carl gave himself mental encouragement. He found he was adding to his load by making discouraging remarks to himself: "If Dalton hears we're stuck, I'll be ruined!" "If Fred tells that story one more time, I'll crack up!" The next time he heard one of these remarks in his head, he simply unloaded it: "No, if Dalton hears we're stuck, I'll be embarrassed (not ruined). And I'll need to be sure he gets the word when we're unstuck." "No, if Fred tells that story one more time, I'll feel annoyed, all right. But I won't crack up."

Carl looked for the humor in the situation. He didn't get sarcastic or tell dark jokes. He just looked for the light side. When Enid met a deadline he realized was unreasonable, for example, Carl brought her a "Wonder Woman" nameplate for her desk. And when time pressure mounted, he posted a feature from a health newsletter (see Figure 8-3).

Carl found ways to work smarter instead of harder. Carl gets to work early and spends twenty minutes planning his day. That twenty minutes saves him hours. He now calculates that he used to "fritter away" a matter of hours in a week looking for ways to stall an unpleasant task. Now when one of those dread tasks shows up on his daily plan, Carl gets it over with first thing. Then he seems energized for the other things on his list. He learned to let go of tasks he had delegated. Oh, he followed up at a designated time, all right. But he stopped fretting and looking over people's shoulders in the meantime. Perhaps most importantly, Carl started saying "No." At one time Carl's phone number was the engineering equivalent to 911. Anyone who needed assistance called Carl. No one needed to twist his arm. He enjoyed helping, and being asked to help boosted his ego. But he finally realized that being 911 added tonnage to his emotional load. Now if helping pushes him close to his personal Plimsoll line, he says, "No."

Figure 8–3
Rush Job Calendar

RUSH JOB CALENDAR

1. Every job is a rush. Everyone wants his job yesterday. With this calendar, someone can order his work on the 7th and have it delivered on the 3rd.

2. Everyone wants his job on Friday so there are three Fridays in every week.

3. There are seven days at the end of the month for those end-of-the-month jobs.

4. There will be no first-of-the-month bills to be paid, as there isn't any 1st. The 10th and the 25th have also been omitted in case you have been asked to pay bills on one of those days.

5. There are no bothersome, nonproductive Saturdays and Sundays. □

Carl practiced deep breathing and muscle relaxation exercises. After an especially trying project meeting, for example, he would retire to the privacy of his own office. There he would close his eyes for about ninety seconds, see a blank slate in his mind, and breathe deeply and slowly. After his ninety second break and a good stretch, he would be relaxed and refreshed—ready to go on to the next thing. He often substituted a brisk walk for a coffee break. And the systematic tensing and relaxing of muscles further helped him unwind.

Carl asserted himself. As with a lot of us, Carl had an uneasy feeling that there was something wrong in simply asking for exactly what he wanted. Yet when he stifled his needs, he often felt drained—even victimized—in the situation. To remain sensitive to other people's feelings and to ask for what he wants as well, he follows the same approach he used in writing the script for his conversation with Brad. (See Chapter Six if you want a review.)

SUMMARY

Project management is subject to The Fatal Law of Gravity: When you are down, everything falls on you. So the project manager's success depends largely on his ability to manage in an environment with many "downers" without getting down himself. These are the first two steps in a strategy that can help.

Step A. Expect conflict and plan how to deal with it

Both the source and the focus of conflict will vary. The source is likely to vary with phases in the project's life cycle. The seven most frequent sources of conflict overall are: schedules, priorities, manpower, technical issues, administration, personality, and costs; The focus will vary with attributes of the team and of the project goals. With an experienced team, the focus of conflict is likely to be within the team itself. With only loosely defined project goals, the focus of conflict will likely be between the team and top management or between the team and the client or both.

Step B. Have stress management techniques in place before the project begins

By paying attention to signals from his body, the project manager can spot stress in time to do something about it. His strategy for coping should include a plan to give himself encouragement; look for humor in the situation; find ways to work smarter instead of harder; practice deep breathing and muscle relaxation exercises; assert himself.

Planning to Handle Conflict

Use the following chart to identify those sources of conflict most likely to be intense during the current phase of your project.

Survey Rankings of Seven Sources of Conflict

	Project Formulation	Build-Up	Main Program	Phase-Out
Schedules	3	2	1	1
Priorities	1	1	4	4
Manpower	4	5	3	3
Technical Issues	6	4	2	6
Administration	2	3	5	7
Personality	7	6	7	2
Cost	5	7	6	5

1. Find the rankings for the current phase of your project.

2. Rank the sources of conflict as you see them.

3. How do your rankings compare with those in the survey?

Top Three Sources
in Survey

Top Three Sources
in Your Ranking

1. _____

1. _____

2. _____

2. _____

3. _____

3. _____

4. If your rankings vary drastically from those in the survey, get a second opinion. Ask a team member or a confidante who has knowledge of the project to rank the sources. How do his rankings compare with your own?

What conflicts in your project up to this point do you suspect of being personality conflicts in disguise?

_____

_____

_____

_____

Which has been your preferred style of dealing with conflict in previous projects (or up to this point in the current project)?

_____ Withdrawal   _____ Forcing

_____ Smoothing   _____ Confrontation

_____ Compromising

Which style will you try to rely on more for the rest of this project? _____

Which style will you rely on less? _____

Use the following chart to find the most likely focus of persistent conflict on

your project. What is the most likely focus? _____

_____

Table 8–7
Attributes of a Project and Focus of Conflict

Experience with Technology	Extent of Agreement on Outcomes	
	Loosely-defined Outcomes	Well-defined Outcomes
High Company Experience	Conflict within Team and Conflict between Team and the Outside Equally High	Higher Conflict within Team
Low Company Experience	Higher Conflict between Team and the Outside	Both Equally Low

Which questions about individual roles are generating conflict for key people in your project?

- Who is asking "Am I in or out?" "Do I belong in this group or not?"

  _____

  _____

  _____

• Who is asking "Am I top or bottom?" "How will the group make decisions?" "How much responsibility, how much influence, how much control will I have?"

_____

_____

_____

• Who is asking "Am I near or far?" "How close should I get?" "How much of myself should I share?" "How much should I care?" "How much could I be hurt?"

_____

_____

_____

Use the following "market analysis" to analyze someone who is stuck on one of those questions about individual roles. Then, use the next worksheet to script an approach to that person.

Market Analysis of Someone Who Is Stuck

☐ The Official Decision-Maker: _____

☐ The Opinion Leader: _____

☐ The Gatekeeper: _____

☐ The Consumer: _____

Personal Style: _____

_____

_____

Relationship with You: _____

_____

_____

Relationships with Other Key People: _____

_____

_____

Pressure to Accept Idea

Job-Related	Other

Pressure to Resist Idea

Job-Related	Other

Script to Use with Someone Who Is Stuck

Key Person _____

Empathy Statement

_____

_____

_____

_____

Connecting Word

_____

Statement of Problem as You See It

_____

_____

_____

_____

_____

Connecting Word

_____

Conclusion (request, call for action, decision)

_____

_____

_____

_____

_____

_____

_____

Managing Stress

1. Answer these questions to help you recognize a stressful situation in time to do something about it.

   • Identify some past situations in which your stress load has gone beyond your personal Plimsoll line:

   _____

   _____

   _____

   _____

   _____

   _____

   _____

   • What signals did you get from your body when you passed (or were approaching) the Plimsoll line?

   _____   _____

   _____   _____

   _____   _____

   • Which of these signals is your body giving you now?

   _____   _____

   _____   _____

   _____   _____

2. Answer these questions to find ways to tell yourself you can handle the situation calmly.

• How can you reply to the negative voices in your head? Write out a response to one of the voices. If the voices are predicting catastrophe (with words like "ruined," "devastated," "disastrous"), you predict control (with phrases like "embarrassed, but . . ," "disappointed, but . . ," "difficult, but. . . ."). Replace each catastrophic word with something that is both more realistic and more manageable.

_____

_____

_____

_____

_____

• What humor do you find in the situation? Would some of this be funny if it were happening to someone else? (Then try to laugh at yourself.) Can you imagine this situation from a scene in a farce? (Keystone Cops? Young Frankenstein?) If you designed a T-shirt for your team, what slogan would be written on it?

• How can you work smarter instead of harder?

Do you spend at least twenty minutes planning each day?
Do you get unpleasant tasks out of the way first?
Do you let go of delegated tasks?
Do you say "No" when you should?

• Have you cleared space in your day for relaxation and exercise?

• Do you assert yourself without being insensitive to others?

9

Facing The Conflict

A Baghdad merchant sent his servant to market, but was surprised to see him return empty-handed. The servant frantically asked his master for the use of a horse so he could escape to Samarra: he had seen Death in the marketplace and been threatened by him. In Samarra he would be safe. The servant soon rode away on a borrowed horse to escape his fate. Feeling greatly unsettled, the merchant then went to the marketplace himself to investigate. The merchant, too, saw Death. But he approached Death head on, "Why did you threaten my servant?" Death replied, looking puzzled, "I didn't mean to look threatening. I was just so surprised to see him here in Baghdad. You see, I have an appointment with him tonight in Samarra."

Some of the things we dread the most are inevitable. Conflict is one of them. More often than not, when we try to escape it, a conflict will seek us out. Our hope, "Ignore it and it will go away," is a vain one in this case. "Ignore it and it will get worse" is more likely.

Even minor disagreements matter when they are frequent or persistent. Perhaps without even realizing it, we "gunny sack" them until they add up to a heavy load. Then we may go under. Or we may transform instantaneously from Mr. or Ms. Nice Guy to Konan the Destroyer.

Perhaps we don't always recognize the major conflicts in time. More likely, we just don't *want* to recognize them; and we look the other way. Often we're afraid we just can't handle them. First we use every avoidance device in the book. When those inevitably fail, we panic.

Avoidance typically magnifies problems; facing them head on typically reduces them. Facing head on isn't the same as facing off. In fact, one element of success is dealing squarely with hostility *without* responding in like kind. And in some cases a project manager must go even a step further. In some cases the real conflict won't confront him directly; so like the Baghdad merchant, he must go out and find it. To handle the conflict effectively, then, the project manager must take these next two steps:

- Step C. Serve as a lightning rod.
- Step D. Excavate the real issues.

In this chapter we'll develop these two steps and see how Carl can take them in his project.

◆ Step C ◆ SERVE AS A LIGHTNING ROD

Conflict management style sets successful project managers apart. One study that compared managers of successful projects with managers of projects that failed (Hill, 1977, pp. 45–61) found that the managers of successful projects

- personally absorbed aggression;
- set an example of listening;
- counseled
- encouraged openness and emotional expression
- served as role models
- paced and controlled potential conflict when possible
- sensed some usefulness in conflict

Notice that in each distinguishing behavior, the high-performing project managers faced the conflict without responding to it in like kind—without taking it personally. Perhaps all of these items are actually subsets of the first: the high performing project managers personally absorbed aggression. But that word "absorb" conjures up a rather frightening picture: a person soaking up more and more hostility with no place to unload it. Overload isn't the answer. So in this chapter we'll use the phrase "serve as a lightning rod" instead. The project manager as lightning rod can take the heat, all right; but then he grounds it so it neither harms him nor its source. How? He can

- put himself on hold;
- screen out distractions
- give it some time;
- respond to both the feeling content and the factual content of the situation.

Let's see how Carl can do these things in his inevitable conflict with Brad Thornton. Remember that Brad is under pressure from his supervisor to withhold support from—even undermine—Carl's project. Sure enough, Brad is challenging and complaining at every turn. And Carl has decided to speak to him about it. Now it would be terrific if Brad immediately fell in line. But what if he explodes? What can Carl do then?

We would rather have things go smoothly, but Carl's opening conversation with Brad could go like this.

Carl: *Brad, I realize Mark doesn't think revised operating standards are worth the effort. And maybe you think common sense is a better guide yourself. Besides, it's hard to be sure what kind of result you'll get from a group effort. Sometimes there are so many compromises nobody is satisfied.*

Brad: *You got that right! This project isn't worth the effort! Like 90 percent of the things we do in this company, it's one big waste of time—mine and everybody else's. Everybody talks about improving productivity. We'd be a lot better off if we stopped talking and just got the work done.*

      My productivity doesn't need improving. I've outproduced the whole lot of you, made the best of my time. Precious little to show for it. I make the best use of my time. Then along you come, a hot-shot Professional Engineer, and waste it. And get paid a fat salary for it!

Carl's approach to Brad could be met with a direct attack. What would he do then?

Put himself on hold

Carl's instinctive reaction would probably be to fight back. He would be tempted to lash out: "I waste *your* time! I wish I had a nickel for every minute of mine *you've* wasted with your whining and complaining!"

It would be a classic case of "one thing led to another." Escalation would be the order of the day. Besides, like it or not, Brad may not have had his say. Interrupting his outburst would prolong it and probably fan the flames. For the time being, Carl will set his own feelings, his own agenda aside. He will give his full attention to Brad.

Screen out distractions

If Carl isn't tempted to fight back, he will probably be tempted to deflect the attack. He may lean toward the telephone hoping for a ring, look out the door searching for a visitor, turn toward the window praying for a bolt of lightning. Anything to draw attention away from the unpleasantness. He might deny it: "Now, Brad, you really don't mean that." He might condemn it: "You shouldn't feel that way!" He might probe: "When did you start feeling this way?" He might change the subject: "Well, on to other things—When does Mark think the first AC-12 will come off the line?"

But in handling conflict, deflection and defection lead to the same place. Whether Carl tries to escape physically or mentally, he'll be on the road to Samarra.

So instead of creating distractions, Carl would screen them out.

- He would sit facing Brad, on the same side of the desk as Brad—not barricaded behind it.
- He would place both feet flat on the ground. Being flat footed averts several problems. Carl can't unconsciously swing his foot nervously. He won't be angling his body to the side; he can face Brad squarely. He won't be drawing that psychological line that leaves Brad on the other side.
- He would lean toward Brad at a 20° or 30° angle. By doing so he would draw a circle that leaves everyone else out.
- He would sit close enough to Brad that he could talk privately but not so close that he would trespass Brad's personal space. Brad, like most of us, probably surrounds himself with a circle of personal space about three feet in radius.

> • He would maintain steady eye contact with Brad. (This isn't the same thing as glaring. A relaxed expression on Carl's face makes the difference.)

By screening out distractions, Carl would be focusing his energy directly on Brad and on the conflict. He would be heading for the marketplace in Baghdad.

Give it some time

Saying the wrong thing would make matters worse. So would saying anything too soon. Carl needs a few seconds to refocus. Brad needs time to finish and to hear himself. So Carl would wait a minimum of ten seconds before he says anything at all. If silence is golden, it is also often awkward. Carl's ten second wait may seem like ten hours to him. Literally counting to ten (but not out loud) would be a good way to help that time pass.

Respond to both the feeling content and the factual content of the situation

Remember that project managers in our survey felt personality conflicts were often disguised as conflict over other issues. Dealing only with the matters of fact can permit those disguises to persist. Dealing with feelings as well as facts can unveil them.

How? Name without blame. Unnamed feelings slow down a project. If they were expressed, positive feelings could give a project a shot in the arm. If they were expressed constructively, negative feelings could clarify confusion or remove a bottleneck. To administer that shot in the arm, to clarify that confusion, to remove that roadblock, a project manager must be able to name another person's feeling and name his own as well. To do that without blame, he must express feelings *as* feelings, not facts. He must accept responsibility for his own feelings. He must avoid being judgmental.

To name another person's feelings, he can use the format, "You seem to feel . . . because. . . ." In responding to Brad, for example, Carl might say, "You seem to feel angry because this project is taking up so much time." Or—more casually—he might say, "Sounds like you're angry about the amount of your time this project takes." Notice that Carl wouldn't claim to be reading Brad's mind. "You seem . . ." and "Sounds like . . ." show his comments are tentative. And he would avoid judgmental words. He would *not* say, for example, "You're just being difficult because you want to make things hard for me!"

To name his own feelings, he can use the format, "When X happens, I feel. . . ." Carl might say to Brad, for example, "When you criticize an idea at a project meeting, I feel frustrated." Notice that Carl would label his feelings as feelings, and he would accept responsibility for them. He would not say, "You make me so angry." (That would put Brad in control of Carl's anger. But whatever Brad does, Carl is responsible for his own reaction—whether it's anger or reason.)

◆ Step D ◆ EXCAVATE THE REAL ISSUES

Conflict that remains below the surface can seep through in many irritating or outright harmful ways: distorted information, withheld information, slipped schedules, unplanned absences from project meetings. The real issues feeding the conflict may be concealed by debris or covered with dust. Now if they are attacked, these concealed issues will simply burrow further underground and continue to pollute the project from a safer distance. Bulldozing would send them further into hiding. So a project manager must handle them gently but firmly—persistently moving aside the debris, gently brushing away the dust—as if these issues were prized artifacts. To excavate these issues, he may

1. treat the surface issue as "real" three times (maybe two is enough);
2. after the third (or second) time, begin to excavate by saying something like, "Sounds like you feel . . . because. . . ." or by using the assertive model;
3. use planning or other aids (like the Linear Responsibility Chart) to make the conflicting issues "visible" to the other parties involved;
4. give loads of support.

Treat the surface issue as "real" three times (maybe two is enough)

Project priorities are real and important issues. Administrative issues are vital to the maintenance of the project; but they can seem like a real drain of energy from the purpose of the project—an understandable source of irritation. And for people juggling several projects and reporting to several chains of command, scheduling is a constant source of stress. Can a project manager assume one of these issues is merely a disguise? No. Can he afford to invest time and energy in one of these issues that is a disguise? No again.

A project manager must necessarily give an issue the benefit of the doubt. At first. But when efforts that should have resolved the issue continue to fail, those efforts are probably directed at a disguise—not a real issue. If a project manager has made only one effort, he probably doesn't have enough information to distinguish one from the other. If he has made five efforts, he probably has more than enough information. (Though he may not want to look at it; or he may not know how.) After two, three, or four failed efforts, he should start excavating.

Suppose Carl has already treated one of Brad's complaints as real three times. Brad has complained about the scheduling of project meetings from the very beginning: the time of day is inconvenient, the meeting location is out of the way. After the first complaint, Carl asked, "Brad, what would work better for you?" But Brad offered no suggestions. He just muttered and sputtered to himself for a while, then sulked for the rest of the meeting. After the second complaint, Carl asked the same question. When he got no response, he went further, "If the time of day poses a continuous problem for you, let's change it. Would right after lunch be more convenient?" Again, Brad muttered and sputtered; but he didn't respond directly to Carl's question. After the third complaint, Carl asked his original question one more time, "What would work better for you?" When he got a nonresponse this time, he again went further, "If it's the location that's the real problem, let's change it. Would the conference room in Building 10 be more convenient?" Again, Brad muttered and sputtered; again he made no specific response.

After the third (or second) time, begin to excavate by saying something like, "Sounds like you feel . . . because. . . ." or by using the assertive model

As his excavation takes him closer and closer to the real issue, it is more and more likely the project manager will need to act as a lightning rod. To the other person, it may feel like the project manager is closing in not just getting closer.

Carl treated the time and location issue as real three times. If the issue *were* real, one of Carl's efforts should have made some difference. But Brad's behavior was no different, so Carl was ready to excavate. Alone with Brad, Carl said, "Brad, it sounds like you feel unhappy because you have to come to project meetings at all—regardless of the time or place."

Predictably, Brad exploded. Carl served as a lightning rod until he was sure Brad had gotten it all out. Then he asserted, "Brad, it sounds like something about this project is really upsetting you. But from where I sit, it doesn't look like the time and location of project meetings is really the important issue. I asked for suggestions three times, and so far you've made none. I can't get you much relief if I don't know what's really going on. So, I'd like you to take a few minutes right now and just level with me."

Use planning or other aids (like the Linear Responsibility Chart) to make the conflicting issues visible to the other parties involved

"Oh, *now* I see!" Those are welcome words to someone who has been struggling to get his point across in a conflict. They are often hard-earned words, as well. Instead of saying "See what I mean?" a project manager is likely to get better results if he literally shows someone what he means instead.

Team members often have different answers to the question "Who talks to whom about what and why (or when)?" Everyone may complain about the old-line bureaucratic structure. But at least they could rely on it for clear-cut answers. In a project the answers aren't so clear. And the subquestion "Who makes the final decision?" is even trickier. A team member (or a project manager, for that matter) who answers that question "I do" only to be overruled is likely to feel both humiliated and hostile. And the team that doesn't bother to answer the question at all can exert a lot of energy trying to satisfy the wrong person. The result can be frustration and anger to the spill-over point.

One way to resolve conflict over questions of procedure or authority is the Linear Responsibility Chart, the most detailed of which assigns responsibilities by individual steps in each project task. Of course, at the outset of a project, it's unlikely that a project manager knows all the tasks—much less all the steps. But that's no reason to wait until confusion develops to chart responsibility. The project manager can begin with the phases in a project life cycle and refine the chart to greater detail when it is possible to do so. Carl has prepared the chart shown in Table 9-1 (pp. 155–156).

Theoretically, the formulation phase of a project life cycle would include activities like these:

1. identify need;
2. develop an initial response plan;
3. test feasibility of initial response;
4. generate alternate strategies to meet response objectives;
5. answer these questions to set parameters—
   • What will the response cost?
   • When will it be ready?

Table 9–1
Linear Responsibility Chart

RESPONSIBILITIES
A. Authorizes
B. Coordinates outside division
C. Supervises
D. Completes
E. Must be consulted
F. Must approve final product/service

Key People

Management
- Bedford Haynes, President
- Edward Dalton, Sr. V.P.
- Walter Pruitt, Engineering Mgr.

Project Team
- Carl White, Engineering
- Brad Thornton, Production
- Enid Schwartz, Methods & Standards
- Jack Thompson, Quality Assurance
- Fred Kemp, Maintenance

Support Staff
- (Not yet assigned)

Users
- Edward Dalton [See Mgt. Col.]
- Mark Johnson, Production
- Chris Latham, Methods & Standards
- Walter Pruitt [See Mgt. Col.]
- Helen Kraus, Quality Assurance
- Jeff Moore, Maintenance

Project Life Cycle
Formulation Phase.

1. Identify need.
2. Develop an initial response plan.
3. Test feasibility of initial response.
4. Generate alternate strategies to meet response objectives.
5. Answer these questions to set parameters:
   - What will the response cost?
   - When will it be ready?
   - What will it do?
   - How will it fit into existing systems?
6. Design tentative project system.
7. Define relationships (interfaces).
8. Identify human and technical resources needed.
9. Assign project manager.

Buildup Phase.

1. Develop project organization.
2. Define final system performance requirements.
3. Develop detailed project plans.
4. Define in detail relationships needed within the project.
5. Define in detail relationships needed between the project system and the outside. (Include transfer of responsibility to user and the reassignment of staff.)

Table 9–1 (continued)

RESPONSIBILITIES
A. Authorizes
B. Coordinates outside division
C. Supervises
D. Completes
E. Must be consulted
F. Must approve final product/service

Key People

Management
- Bedford Haynes, President
- Edward Dalton, Sr. V.P.
- Walter Pruitt, Engineering Mgr.

Project Team
- Carl White, Engineering
- Brad Thornton, Production
- Enid Schwartz, Methods & Standards
- Jack Thompson, Quality Assurance
- Fred Kemp, Maintenance

Support Staff
- (Not yet assigned)

Users
- Edward Dalton [See Mgt. Col.]
- Mark Johnson, Production
- Chris Latham, Methods & Standards
- Walter Pruitt [See Mgt. Col.]
- Helen Kraus, Quality Assurance
- Jeff Moore, Maintenance

Project Life Cycle

Buildup Phase.
6. Identify support needed.
7. Develop policies and procedures.
8. Complete staffing.

Main Program Phase.
1. Update detailed project plans.
2. Verify performance standards.
3. Develop, produce, and install product or service.
4. Test.
5. Feedback results and act on them.
6. Identify support needed during operation.
7. Develop users' manual.
8. Monitor operation by user.
9. Integrate product or service into user's system.
10. Evaluate operation.

Phase-Out.
1. Refine plans to transfer responsibility from project team to user.
2. Transfer responsibility.
3. Establish followup system.
4. Explore and report lessons learned.
5. Reassign staff

- What will it do?
- How will it fit into existing systems?
6. design tentative project system;
7. define relationships (interfaces);
8. identify human and technical resources needed;
9. assign project manager.

If this project were "by the book" a lot of footwork would have been done before Carl's assignment as project manager. In fact, Ed Dalton identified (or perceived) the need and developed an initial response plan in about thirty seconds. And within an hour Carl was the project manager—drafted along with the other team members. Carl's team is in an awkward—but not that unusual— spot: they will begin with the third activity of the formulation phase—testing the feasibility of a response that has already been mandated.

Carl could have simply mandated further—moved right on to developing a project system. But what if Brad Thornton turned out to be right? What if the project would not be worthwhile? Is Carl's job simply to properly space the rivets on the bridge or is it to help decide if the bridge is worth building? Carl and Walter agreed that Carl's team should test feasibility and feed back to Ed Dalton before proceeding further.

Since the project hasn't begun "by the book," can a Linear Responsibility Chart be of any value to Carl? Carl has quickly sketched in some assignments on the chart shown in Table 9-2.

Now he wishes he had taken the time to set up the chart before his first encounter with Brad Thornton. Now he realizes the following:

- Some important footwork has been left out. Ed Dalton *may* have perceived the need accurately. Revised operating standards *might* be an appropriate response. But at this point, Carl must show Brad's objections some respect. There isn't enough data to dismiss them.
- He doesn't need any data to realize that Ed Dalton must be satisfied. Regardless of the pressure Brad is under from his boss, regardless of the disinterest of Carl's boss, a vice-president wants something done. This chart can bring that point home to Brad.
- Brad can have many opportunities in this formulation phase to act on his concerns if they are real. Excavation

Table 9-2
Carl's Tentative Linear Responsibility Chart

RESPONSIBILITIES

A. Authorizes
B. Coordinates outside division
C. Supervises
D. Completes
E. Must be consulted
F. Must approve final product/service

Project Life Cycle	Management			Project Team					Support Staff	Users					
Key People	Bedford Haynes, President	Edward Dalton, Sr. V.P.	Walter Pruitt, Engineering Mgr.	Carl White, Engineering	Brad Thornton, Production	Enid Schwartz, Methods & Standards	Jack Thompson, Quality Assurance	Fred Kemp, Maintenance	(Not yet assigned)	Edward Dalton [See Mgt. Col.]	Mark Johnson, Production	Chris Latham, Methods & Standards	Walter Pruitt [See Mgt. Col.]	Helen Kraus, Quality Assurance	Jeff Moore, Maintenance
Formulation Phase.															
1. Identify need.		A,D													
2. Develop an initial response plan.	E,F	A,D	E												
3. Test feasibility of initial response.		E	E	B,C							E	E		E	E
4. Generate alternate strategies to meet response objectives.				B,C							E	E		E	E
5. Answer these questions to set parameters:				B,C											
What will the response cost?				B,C											
When will it be ready?				B,C											
What will it do?				B,C											
How will it fit into existing systems?				B,C											
6. Design tentative project system.	E,F			B,C											
7. Define relationships (interfaces).				B,C											
8. Identify human and technical resources needed.				B,C											
9. Assign project manager.															
Buildup Phase.															
1. Develop project organization.				B,C											

2. Define final system performance requirements.

3. Develop detailed project plans.

4. Define in detail relationships needed within the project.

5. Define in detail relationships needed between the project system and the outside. (Include transfer of responsibility to user and the reassignment of staff.)

6. Identify support needed.

7. Develop policies and procedures.

8. Complete staffing.

Main Program Phase.

1. Update detailed project plans.

2. Verify performance standards.

3. Develop, produce, and install product or service.

4. Test.

5. Feedback results and act on them.

6. Identify support needed during operation.

7. Develop users' manual.

8. Monitor operation by user.

9. Integrate product or service into user's system.

10. Evaluate operation.

Phase-Out.

1. Refine plans to transfer responsibility from project team to user.

2. Transfer responsibility.

3. Establish followup system.

4. Explore and report lessons learned.

5. Reassign staff

may uncover real doubts about the value of the project, real questions about cost effectiveness, real concerns about the way the project will affect systems already in place. If these real issues surface, Brad can help the group deal with them as they test feasibility, generate alternate strategies, answer questions about parameters, design the tentative system, define relationships. Showing Brad this chart, Carl can assure him these issues will be dealt with. In fact, he can assign Carl primary responsibility for developing some recommendations.

Give loads of support

One consultant writes about the importance of support in a work relationship "even if the client is seven feet tall, has scales and breathes fire. . . ." (Block, 1981, p. 69). In fact, behind the facade, underneath the bravado, most people do want to feel secure, to feel worthwhile, and to receive encouragement. Too often, though, managers confuse support with agreement. The natural result, then, is the withholding of support during a disagreement—when it is needed the most.

Though Carl disagrees with Brad's abrasive behavior, he will make a special effort to give Brad moral support. He will listen attentively and show understanding. He will refrain from judgment. He will use whatever is useful in Brad's comments despite Brad's abrasive delivery. He will give Brad regular feedback and—whenever it's at all feasible—he will give Brad praise.

SUMMARY

Conflict is one of those inevitable things that many project managers dread. Ignoring it just won't work. And if a project manager tries, he might just let the pressure build up until he explodes. But to face conflict, a project manager must sometimes find it first—not contrive it, just find it if it's there. So to face conflict directly, a project manager must take these additional steps:

Step A. Serve as a lightning rod

The project manager's objective in this step is to take the heat himself, then ground it so it will not harm anyone. The Project Manager as lightning rod will put his own feelings on hold, screen out distractions, and give the lightning some time to run its course. Then he will respond to both the feelings and the facts in the situation.

Step B. Excavate the real issues

When the real issues causing conflict are buried, the project manager's job is more complicated. It's not safe to assume any issue is a disguise, so he will take an issue at face value two or three times. But when efforts that should work continue to fail, he will begin to excavate, he will use visual aids to make the conflict visible, and he will give support.

Being a "Lightning Rod"

Briefly describe a project conflict during which your effort to deal with the situation calmly was met with a direct attack.

_____

_____

_____

_____

_____

How did you respond to the attack? If you remember your exact behavior and your exact words, write them out.

_____

_____

_____

_____

_____

Rate your response on how well it compares with the characteristics of managers of successful projects (Hill, 1977, pp. 45–61). If your response fully demonstrated a characteristic, give yourself a 5 for that characteristic. If your response totally omitted a characteristic, give yourself a 0 for that characteristic.

_____ Personally absorbed aggression (served as a "lightning rod")
_____ Set an example of listening
_____ Counseled
_____ Encouraged openness and emotional expression
_____ Served as a role model
_____ Paced and controlled potential conflict when possible
_____ Sensed some usefulness in the conflict

Now visualize that situation happening again. Mentally rehearse the way you would do the following:

1. Put yourself on hold.
   - Picture yourself remaining quiet, even if your instinctive reaction is to lash out.
   - See your mind as a blank screen with your thoughts, your feelings erased.

2. Screen out distractions.
   - Picture yourself facing the other person in the conflict, sitting about three feet apart on the same side of the desk.
   - Picture yourself leaning toward the other person at a 20° or 30° angle with your feet flat on the ground.
   - Picture yourself making direct eye contact with a relaxed expression on your face.

3. Give it some time. Picture yourself remaining quiet and relaxed for 10 seconds after the other person has finished speaking.

4. Respond to both the feeling content and the factual content of the situation. Complete the blanks in this statement. Then picture (and hear) yourself saying it to the other person in the conflict.

"Sounds like you feel _____ because _____

_____ ."

Excavating the Issue

1. Identify three ways you could treat the issue as it was originally presented as real.

_____

_____

_____

_____

_____

_____

_____

2. Fill in the following Assertive Script to show how you would begin to excavate if the conflict persists.

3. Fill in a Linear Responsibility Chart for your project so far. (You may want to make this a team project.)

What features of your chart surprise you? _____

_____

_____

_____

What else did you learn from it?

_____

_____

_____

_____

_____

4. List three to five specific ways you can give another person in the project support without agreeing with him.

_____

_____

_____

_____

_____

_____

_____

_____

_____

_____

Assertive Script

Key Person _____

Empathy Statement

_____

_____

_____

_____

Connecting Word

_____

Statement of Problem as You See It

_____

_____

_____

_____

_____

Connecting Word

_____

Conclusion (request, call for action, decision)

_____

_____

_____

_____

_____

_____

_____

Table 9–3
Blank Linear Responsibility Chart

RESPONSIBILITIES
A. Authorizes
B. Coordinates outside division
C. Supervises
D. Completes
E. Must be consulted
F. Must approve final product/service

Key People / Project Life Cycle	Management			Project Team					Support Staff	Users					
	Bedford Haynes, President	Edward Dalton, Sr. V.P.	Walter Pruitt, Engineering Mgr.	Carl White, Engineering	Brad Thornton, Production	Enid Schwartz, Methods & Standards	Jack Thompson, Quality Assurance	Fred Kemp, Maintenance	(Not yet assigned)	Edward Dalton [See Mgt. Col.]	Mark Johnson, Production	Chris Latham, Methods & Standards	Walter Pruitt [See Mgt. Col.]	Helen Kraus, Quality Assurance	Jeff Moore, Maintenance
Formulation Phase.															
1. Identify need.															
2. Develop an initial response plan.															
3. Test feasibility of initial response.															
4. Generate alternate strategies to meet response objectives.															
5. Answer these questions to set parameters:															
What will the response cost?															
When will it be ready?															
What will it do?															
How will it fit into existing systems?															
6. Design tentative project system.															
7. Define relationships (interfaces).															
8. Identify human and technical resources needed.															
9. Assign project manager.															
Buildup Phase.															
1. Develop project organization.															

2. Define final system performance requirements.

3. Develop detailed project plans.

4. Define in detail relationships needed within the project.

5. Define in detail relationships needed between the project system and the outside. (Include transfer of responsibility to user and the reassignment of staff.)

6. Identify support needed.

7. Develop policies and procedures.

8. Complete staffing.

Main Program Phase.

1. Update detailed project plans.

2. Verify performance standards.

3. Develop, produce, and install product or service.

4. Test.

5. Feedback results and act on them.

6. Identify support needed during operation.

7. Develop users' manual.

8. Monitor operation by user.

9. Integrate product or service into user's system.

10. Evaluate operation.

Phase-Out.

1. Refine plans to transfer responsibility from project team to user.

2. Transfer responsibility.

3. Establish followup system.

4. Explore and report lessons learned.

5. Reassign staff

10

*R*esponding to the *C*onflict

The feng-huang is an ancient Chinese bird that appears only when reason prevails. Nobody has seen a feng-huang in a long, long time.

For a long, long time people have responded to emotional threat in the same way they instinctively responded to physical danger. (See Figure 10-1)

But when it's applied to an emotional conflict, that win-lose approach invariably leads to a lose-lose conclusion. The features of an effective response to emotional threat are in sharp contrast to the features of the traditional response to physical danger (See Figure 10-2).

Figure 10–1
Traditional Features of Success Strategy with
Physical Conflict

Adrenalin: The surge of adrenalin ("Fight or Flight") is functional.
Best Peace Strategy: To show strength • Stay on guard. • Leave no vulnerable position.
Physical Stance: Square off to display strength and intimidate opponent.
Mental Stance: • Size up the opponent. • Evaluate the opponent's strengths and   weaknesses.
Most Valuable Data: Pay attention to verifiable fact.
Control: To limit the conflict use • Containment. • Divide and conquer strategy.
Speed: • Be swift. • Be sure.

So often we confuse force with strength, weakness with gentleness. But it takes strength to handle others gently in a hostile setting. Suppose a beloved family member were returning home after major surgery and needed to be carried from the car to the house. Who would you choose to help? Not the physically weak person who would tremble under the load. You would choose the most fit person—the one strong enough to carry the weight gently.

The most fit project manager is also strong enough to carry the weight gently in an emotionally loaded situation. To handle with care, he can take this next step: Step E. Look for win–win alternatives.

Only if win–win alternatives repeatedly fail will he shift his strategy. Even then, he will not be punitive. But as humanely as

Figure 10–2
Physical Conflict vs. Emotional Conflict

Success Strategy for Physical Conflict	Success Strategy for Emotional Conflict
Adrenalin: The surge of adrenalin ("Fight or Flight") is functional.	**Adrenalin:** The "Fight or Flight" response is nonfunctional—even damaging. It can increase blood pressure and pulse rate, for example, with no outlet.
Best Peace Strategy: To show strength • Stay on guard. • Leave no vulnerable position.	**Best Peace Strategy:** To show strength • Let down guard. • Show confidence by being open to vulnerability.
Physical Stance: Square *off* to display strength and intimidate opponent.	**Physical Stance:** Square *away* to establish equality and invite the other person.
Mental Stance: • Size up the opponent. • Evaluate the opponent's strengths and weaknesses.	**Mental Stance:** Reflect nonjudgmentally.
Most Valuable Data: Pay attention to verifiable fact.	**Most Valuable Data:** Pay attention to "fuzzies."
Control: To limit the conflict use • Containment. • "Divide and conquer" strategy.	**Control:** Limit conflict through • Opening up. • Exposing vulnerability.
Speed: • Be swift. • Be sure.	**Speed:** • Pace the conflict. • Individualize the response.

possible he will take this remaining step: Step F. Cut his losses when necessary.

◆ Step E ◆ LOOK FOR WIN-WIN ALTERNATIVES

Project managers don't typically wear rose-colored glasses. (Well, maybe while making initial time and cost estimates.) Those glasses don't help a bit in the search for win-win alternatives, anyway. They only postpone facing some hard facts until it may be too late. On the other hand, blinders won't do any good, either. They just make it easy to give up too soon—to turn gloomy expectations into self-fulfilling prophecies.

What will help? A positive approach in which the project manager can

- do the doable;
- build on his earlier market analysis;
- use the assertive model;
- look at things right side up;
- picture things going well;
- identify priorities and verbalize them.

Do the doable

Don't try to teach ducks to sing. It will only frustrate you and confuse the ducks.

Carl is investing a lot of time and energy in Brad the Complainer. What will be the payoff? Will Brad become a cheerful, enthusiastic group member—a supporter Carl can count on? Probably not doable. Will Brad become a productive team member? That should be doable. If it's not, Carl will take the steps we'll look at later to cut his losses.

Build on his earlier market analysis

Carl will try only to do the doable. And his earlier market analysis can tell him what conditions would meet Brad's criteria for a win-win solution. You can review the analysis in Figure 10-3.

Use the assertive model

The market analysis became the basis for the assertive response shown in Figure 10-4.

Notice, again, how Carl (1) used Brad's strongest job-related reason to resist as the main point of an empathy statement; (2) incorporated Brad's strongest job-related reason to give support in a statement of the problem; and (3) accommodated Brad's nonjob-related pressures in a course of action.

Look at things right side up

In a topsy-turvey environment the most likely view of things is upside down. But a project manager can set things right again when he separates people and problems, when he concentrates on outcomes instead of positions, when he avoids "catastrophizing."

One upside down approach is to attack a person instead of a problem. True, a person sometimes appears to *be* the problem. But if he is ever to see a solution, the project manager must look at the

Figure 10–3
Carl's Earlier Market Analysis of Brad

☐ The Official Decision-Maker: <u>Brad Thornton</u>
   (For this situation)
☐ The Opinion Leader: _____

☐ The Gatekeeper: _____

☐ The Consumer: _____

Personal Style: <u>Capable, But surly and sarcastic. Seems more interested in complaining than in problem solving.</u>

Relationship with You: <u>Not much contact. I have said "Good morning" to Brad in hallway. He walked on without acknowledging.</u>

Relationships with Other Key People: <u>Other relationships don't seem any better. Possible exception is Enid Schwartz. Brad doesn't make negative remarks after Enid's input. Did I even see him nod in agreement once?</u>

Pressure to Accept Idea

Job-Related	Other
* Brad is capable. Probably doesn't want to be <u>seen</u> as contributor to failure.	* If he believes his behavior <u>looks</u> uncooperative he may have some need to maintain esteem with Enid.

Pressure to Resist Idea

Job-Related	Other
* Brad's boss Mark Johnson will put pressure on Brad to undermine the idea of standards. * Brad may actually believe common sense works better than formal standards anyway. * Brad doesn't have confidence in team products.	* Seems to be contentious by nature. * May use negativism to build himself up in Enid's eyes.

Figure 10–4
Carl's Assertive Response to Brad

Key Person *Brad Thornton*

Empathy Statement

Brad, I realize Mark doesn't think revised operating standards are worth the effort. And maybe you think common sense is a better guide yourself. Besides, it's hard to be sure what kind of result you'll get from a group effort. Sometimes there are so many compromises nobody is satisfied.

Connecting Word

But...

Statement of Problem as You See It

...all eyes are on us now. Ed Dalton has given this project high priority. And Bedford Haynes is keeping a watchful eye on it. We would each be hurt by a high visibility project that floundered. And I'm afraid we will flounder if we don't get these control issues settled and get on with it.

Connecting Word

So...

Conclusion (request, call for action, decision)

I'd like for you to help in one of two ways:

1. When you believe an idea won't work, please just jot your objections down and talk to me about them individually right after the team meeting. If there's a problem you and I can't work out, then we can bring it up with the team.

Or

2. If you foresee a problem at the upcoming team meeting, maybe you and Enid could discuss it first. She could probably help generate some solutions to present to the group.

problem and the person separately first. Sometimes it's only necessary to separate the person from the situation. Sometimes it's necessary to separate the person from his own behavior.

A manager complains, "If I just had a halfway decent staff, this project would be finished on time." He sees his staff, not schedule slippage as the problem. A team leader lashes out, "If you would just get off my back, I could work this out!" He sees "you," not his difficulty concentrating, as the problem. These blurred pictures fail to separate the people from the problem, and they bring no solution into focus. Will the manager, for example, solve the problem by firing his entire staff? Probably not.

Several times Carl has caught himself thinking, "If it weren't for Brad, we could get things moving!" And he realized that view of the situation would lead only to more frustration—not to a solution. So he refocused his picture by answering these questions:

Q. *What is happening that I wish were* not *happening?*

A. *We are losing time with too much debate over priorities and over administrative issues.*

Q. *What is* not *happening that I wish* were *happening?*

A. *We are not commiting time and resources to a firm project schedule.*

Q. *What would need to happen in order for me to say "This situation is no longer a problem"?*

A. —*We would need to have a list of objectives with agreed-upon priorities assigned to each one.*
  —*We would need to have interfaces described in writing and agreed upon.*
  —*We would need to have a tentative design for the project system with needed resources identified.*

Carl's right side up view of the problem leads to some specific objectives which, in turn, will lead to some changes in the way he manages project meetings.

And to deal with Brad, Carl will have to go a step further: He will need to separate Brad from Brad's own behavior. He will need to remember he can dislike Brad's caustic remarks without necessarily disliking Brad. He can discourage Brad's disruptive behavior without necessarily discouraging Brad himself.

Another upside down approach is to confuse outcomes with positions. It's easy for people to quickly lock into positions about *how* something will get done. *What* will get done often pales in comparison. Maybe some people remember who won the World Championship Chess Tournament in 1972. But many people who have forgotten the outcome remember the chaos. First Fischer asked for a delay while he complained about the size of the purse. Then he sent a second to represent him. Next Spassky demanded a written apology. Eventually the games started but were interrupted by charges and countercharges of chemical cheating and use of electronic devices. The environment wasn't suitable, the players needed a private room, and on and on. It's tough to interpret Spassky's refusal to show up after the twenty-first game. Was it an admission that he couldn't beat Fischer at playing chess? Or was it an admission that he couldn't beat Fischer at playing the brat?

Whether the arena is chess or project management, the outcome is the same. When people lock into a contest over positions or methods, the Biggest Brat often wins. The other team members and the project itself suffer.

A third upside down approach is "catastrophizing." "We'll *never* get this done!" "This is going to be a disaster!" "This project is driving me crazy!" Those are ways to depict inconvenience, difficulty, or frustration as catastrophes instead of manageable obstacles. "We'll get behind schedule unless we. . . ." "This is a tough one." "I'm feeling frustrated right now." These are ways to paint a realistic picture.

Picture things going well

Everybody's mom used to call this daydreaming. Targeted toward a specific objective, psychologists now call it visionary analysis. In preparing for the Summer Olympics, James Robinson, a premier middle-distance runner ran a winning race again and again—in his head. He mentally rehearsed every split second—every breath, every step. And Robinson wasn't alone. Visualization and imagery is one of the three steps sports psychologist Robert Nideffer recommends to help athletes to maintain peak performance without pressing too hard. (Keister, 1984, pp. 18–24). Not a bad objective for the rest of us in handling conflict, either.

Often we invest much time and energy in detailed descriptions of what ails a situation. But it's difficult to move on to something better unless we can describe what "better" is. To develop a clear picture of "better" a project manager can take these steps.

- First, he should picture things going just like he wants them to. He should ask the questions: "How do I know things are happening the way I want them to?" "What do I feel, see, taste, hear, smell, that tell me I have what I want?" Then he should write down *detailed* answers to these questions.
- Next, he should enroll the support of others. He should tell other people what his objectives are and what their supporting roles are in his mental moving picture. He should spell out exactly what they can do to help and ask them for their commitment to do it.
- Finally, he should deal with obstacles positively. If a voice in his head says "It can't work." He won't simply respond "Why not?" Instead he will respond more positively with "But what if it would work? What would happen then?"

Identify priorities and verbalize them

Too often people compromise in a conflict until everyone feels equally dissatisfied. A prepared project manager knows ahead of time what the "must-haves" and what the "nice-to-haves" are. He will not choose to give up a must-have. But he will rank order nice-to-haves and give up the least important of these when he needs to compromise. He can rank order by asking himself the following:

- "Which of these features would add the most value to the project?"
- "Which of these would add the least value?"

◆ Step F ◆   CUT LOSSES WHEN NECESSARY

"We can't quit now. We've invested too much in this project to give it up."

That's what an elder in Carl's church said at some point before the antique pipe organ offered as a free gift cost the church over a million dollars. First, the session felt it was unethical to accept such a treasure free. So they gave the donor church a token $25,000. Then there were additional costs to have the organ dissembled and moved. Next they agreed to pay $100,000 to have it reconstructed in the receiving church. But $200,000 later the job still wasn't finished. The old organ room wasn't suitable; they built another. The old carpet wasn't acoustically correct; they replaced it. Six years and over one million dollars later, the membership finally insisted that the project to install the free gift be abandoned: it was simply costing too much. Now they have purchased a new organ at an installed price of $500,000.

"I can't give up on him now. I've invested too much time in him for that."

Same song, second verse.

Like many of us Carl has heard—over and over—the old maxim, "Things always turn out for the best." Now that he's an experienced project manager, he can't help wonder if the person who coined that expression was really paying attention. He doesn't, like one pessimist, actually consider Murphy an optimist. On the other hand, some investments of time and energy have seemed like sink holes: they take and take and give nothing back. He'd like to be able to identify a sink hole as soon as possible and then stop pouring time, money, and energy into it.

Carl has invested a lot of time, energy, and emotion in an effort to develop Brad into a productive team member. How much is enough? How much attention can he give Brad without abandoning the other team members? We'll continue to hope for the best. But Brad's behavior *could* cost the group more over a period of time than his participation could possibly be worth. How could Carl cut his losses? He could

- keep a mental "tickler file" of the little things that don't fit;
- follow the Rule of Two (or Three);
- have a system in place for cutting back his investment.

Keep a mental "tickler file" of the little things that don't fit
Four score and seven years ago our fathers brought forth forth on this continent a new nation, conceived in liberty. . . .

It's easy to see what's expected instead of what's real. Did you spot the two *forth*'s in the opening statement of this paragraph? Or did you read only one—what you expected to see.

When the words and the behavior don't match, believe the behavior—even if it's the words you *want* to believe. A father asked his children at dinner if they would like to join him for an outing on Saturday. The ten-year old's face lit up, he jumped up and down, and he squealed, "Hurray!" The twelve-year old leaned toward her father, eyes opened wide, and with a big grin agreed, "Sure, Dad. Great!" The fifteen-year old looked toward the floor momentarily but didn't speak. When his father said, "How about you?" the teenager turned toward the window without making eye contact and muttered "Yeah. . . . O.K." Would the fifteen year old *like* to join his father for the outing? No way. He just may go along rather than put forth any effort to rock the boat.

A project manager asked, "Do we agree that this is the best course of action?" One team member said, "I agree, the best." The second team member echoed, "The best." The third and the fourth answered likewise. The fifth shuffled in his chair and said, "Well, it ought to work." Does the fifth member agree? Probably not. He didn't voice an objection that would rock the boat. But his response breaks the pattern of enthusiastic agreement—breaks it just enough to signal the project manager that something doesn't fit.

By ignoring the break in pattern, the project manager would most likely be accepting passive resistance—the beginning of a hidden sink hole.

Not all sink holes are hidden. Some of them are right there out in the open. But the behavior is so out of field that the project manager simply "doesn't believe his eyes (or his ears)." A team member once blatantly announced to his project manager, "I hate the sight of your boss. And I'll do anything to make him look bad—including jamming up this project." The project manager assumed the team member was making a bad joke and wrote off many danger signals to the man's "crazy sense of humor." Many frustrating days later, the project manager was presented with irrefutable evidence that the team member was living up to his word—he was sabotaging the project.

Follow the Rule of Two (or Three)

Of course a project manager would prefer to cut his losses before they are costly. Sometimes the project manager won't recognize an inconsistency right away. But the second or third time it occurs, he should address it directly.

For example, the first time Carl asked Fred Kemp if he had gotten a firm time commitment from Fred's supervisor, Fred replied, "Mark hasn't tied up my time lately." It was several hours later that Carl realized Fred hadn't really answered his question. So he called Fred up and asked him again. Fred's response was the same, "Mark hasn't tied up my time lately." This time Carl persisted, "Fred, I realize Mark hasn't delayed your coming to project meetings lately.

That's an improvement, but it doesn't go far enough. I want to deal with the problem head on. Have you actually talked to Mark about his commitment of your time to this project?"

Have a system *for cutting back the investment of money, of time, of effort, and of ego*

The old management slogan "Plan your work and work your plan" applies here. When something major goes wrong at work, people are likely to go through the classic stages of grief: denial, anger, bargaining, depression, and—hopefully—acceptance. These emotions can be immobilizing. People in the throes of these emotions after the loss of a loved one are vulnerable to other losses: loss of self-esteem, and being taken advantage of (emotionally and financially) among them. A project manager in the throes of these emotions after he recognizes a major loss on the job is also vulnerable to other losses: loss of self-esteem and being taken advantage of among them.

People who have planned ahead how they will handle the loss of a loved one are protected. They can turn to their written plan and take the action steps one by one. Even taking the action steps will be difficult, of course; but they took care of the most difficult steps—the decisions—when they could think more clearly. Project managers who have planned ahead how they will handle loss at work are protected. They can turn to their written plan and take the action steps one by one. Even taking the action steps will be difficult, of course; but they took care of the most difficult steps— the decisions—when they could think more clearly.

The project manager's plan should answer these questions:

- How much money will he invest before he sees some return?
- How much time will he allow a problem to consume before he follows another course of action (asks that the employee be reassigned or fired, for example)?
- How much energy and ego will he invest before he is satisfied he has "given it his best shot"? (How will he limit preoccupation with the loss at work? How will he limit spillover of the problem into his personal life?)

SUMMARY

People instinctively respond to emotional threat in the same way they have traditionally responded to physical danger. But when it's applied to an emotional conflict, that traditional win-lose approach inevitably leads to a lose-lose conclusion.

But the most emotionally fit project manager will not retaliate. He will handle with care by taking these steps:

Step E. Look for win-win alternatives

The project manager can lay the necessary groundwork if he identifies what's realistically doable, builds on his earlier market analysis, and uses the assertive model. He can resist the punitive sideroads if he looks at things right side up, pictures things going well, and identifies and verbalizes priorities.

Step F. Cut losses when necessary

We may all hope for the best, but it's a good idea to be prepared for the worst. If a project manager is unprepared to deal with loss, he will be vulnerable to many more. He is more likely to anticipate loss when he keeps a mental "tickler file" of the things that go wrong. He is more likely to avert the loss if he follows the Rule of Two and faces it head on. And he can cushion the blow of a loss, when one does occur, if he already has a system in place for cutting back his investment.

Looking at Your Response to Conflict

Briefly describe a conflict situation in which you felt under attack. (You may want to review the situation you described under "Being a Lightning Rod.")

_____

_____

_____

_____

Now circle the paragraphs in the following chart that describe your response.

Physical Conflict vs. Emotional Conflict

Success Strategy for Physical Conflict	Success Strategy for Emotional Conflict
Adrenalin: The surge of adrenalin ("Fight or Flight") is functional.	**Adrenalin:** The "Fight or Flight" response is nonfunctional—even damaging. It can increase blood pressure and pulse rate, for example, with no outlet.
Best Peace Strategy: To show strength • Stay on guard. • Leave no vulnerable position.	**Best Peace Strategy:** To show strength • Let down guard. • Show confidence by being open to vulnerability.
Physical Stance: Square *off* to display strength and intimidate opponent.	**Physical Stance:** Square *away* to establish equality and invite the other person.
Mental Stance: • Size up the opponent. • Evaluate the opponent's strengths and weaknesses.	**Mental Stance:** Reflect nonjudgmentally.
Most Valuable Data: Pay attention to verifiable fact.	**Most Valuable Data:** Pay attention to "fuzzies."
Control: To limit the conflict use • Containment. • "Divide and conquer" strategy.	**Control:** Limit conflict through • Opening up. • Exposing vulnerability.
Speed: • Be swift. • Be sure.	**Speed:** • Pace the conflict. • Individualize the response.

How many paragraphs did you circle under physical conflict? _____

How many did you circle under emotional conflict? _____

Describe three things you would do differently if you were to relive this situation:

_____

_____

_____

_____

_____

Looking for Win-Win Alternatives

1. Write out the outcomes you are hoping for in this conflict. Are you trying to teach ducks to sing? Go back and rate the outcomes as doable or undoable.

Check One		Outcomes
Doable	Undoable	

2. If you have done an earlier market analysis of this situation, review it now. If you have not, do a market analysis here using the worksheet on the next page.

Market Analysis Worksheet

- ❑ The Official Decision-Maker: _____
- ❑ The Opinion Leader: _____
- ❑ The Gatekeeper: _____
- ❑ The Consumer: _____

Personal Style: _____

_____

_____

Relationship with You: _____

_____

_____

Relationships with Other Key People: _____

_____

_____

Pressure to Accept Idea

Job-Related	Other

Pressure to Resist Idea

Job-Related	Other

3. If you have developed an earlier assertive statement for this situation, review it now. If you have not, write an assertive script here using the following worksheet. Remember

- Use the strongest job-related pressure to resist in your statement of the other person's point of view.
- Incorporate the strongest job-related reason to support in the statement of the problem as you see it.
- Accommodate as many nonjob-related pressures as you can in the course of action you propose.

Assertive Script Worksheet

Key Person _____

Empathy Statement

_____

_____

_____

_____

Connecting Word

_____

Statement of Problem as You See It

_____

_____

_____

_____

_____

Connecting Word

_____

Conclusion (request, call for action, decision)

_____

_____

_____

_____

_____

_____

_____

_____

Look at things right side up

Begin by answering these questions to separate the people and the situation:

What *is* happening that you wish *were not* happening?

_____

_____

_____

_____

_____

_____

What *is not* happening that you wish *were* happening?

_____

_____

_____

_____

What would need to happen in order for you to say "This situation is no longer a problem"?

_____

_____

_____

_____

Now separate *what* needs to be done from *how* it might get done.

Describe the "how's" you have locked into that might keep you from reaching the "what."

_____

_____

_____

_____

_____

_____

Next distinguish between your emotions and reality. Rewrite some of the catastrophic things you think or say about the situation to realistically depict the situation as more manageable.

Catastrophic Statement	Realistic Description
_____	_____
_____	_____
_____	_____
_____	_____
_____	_____
_____	_____

Picture the situation turning out well

Describe the details you see that confirm things are going right—what you feel, what you see, what you taste, what you hear, what you smell.

_____

_____

_____

_____

_____

_____

Identify your priorities and verbalize them

List the absolute must-haves here.

_____

_____

_____

_____

_____

List the "nice-to-haves" here. Rank them from one (would add the most value) to X (would add the least value).

_____

_____

_____

_____

_____

_____

Cutting Your Losses

What little things haven't fit?

List the inconsistencies that could be signs of resistance or alienation.

_____   _____

_____   _____

_____   _____

_____   _____

_____   _____

_____   _____

Follow the Rule of Two (or Three)

Write out your statement to confront an inconsistency the second or third time that it occurs.

_____

_____

_____

_____

When and how can you withdraw your investment if the losses become too great?

- How much money will you invest before you see a return? _____
  What will you do to halt your investment?

  _____

  _____

  _____

  _____

- How much time will you allow the problem to consume before you

   take another course of action? _____

- What other course of action will you take?

   _____

   _____

   _____

   _____

- How will you limit preoccupation with the losses at work?

   _____

   _____

   _____

   _____

- How will you limit spillover of the problem into your personal life?

   _____

   _____

   _____

   _____

   _____

✦ Key IV ✦ PROVIDE FOR THE ROUTINE "CARE AND FEEDING" OF THE PROJECT TEAM

Highlights: The Cases of Betty Ashford, Dan Smith, Carl White, and Alan Lord

A successful project manager must do a balancing act: He must constantly balance his investment of energy in completing the task with his investment of energy in caring for his team. If a project manager invests in the task alone, his team may fall apart before the task is completed. Or dissonance may result in time and cost overruns. If a project manager invests in the team alone he may nurture a group of very happy low performers.

Misguided or out-of-balance investment in the project can propel a project manager toward one of four bad ends: *groupthink, burnout, demolition,* or *collapse.*

A positive investment of energy in the team by itself would lead to groupthink, a highly cohesive state of striving for consensus. Groupthink produces poor technical decisions made by a very loyal group. Betty Ashford's highly cohesive project team is at risk to groupthink—especially since it has been subject to resented interference from the outside.

A positive investment of energy in the task by itself would lead to burnout. Burnout is the outcome of intense individual effort toward the task without team support. By-products of burnout include the dissolution of the team, turnover, absenteeism, and high rates of stress-related illnesses. Dan Smith's project is at risk to burnout. Dan's project relies heavily on formal planning and formal controls. It would be easy for Dan and his team to focus so intently on technical aspects of the task that they simply ignore each other.

Misguided or negative energy for the team by itself would lead to demolition. Like groupthink, demolition leads to a bad technical decision or product. But the source of demolition is different: Demolition stems from lack of cohesiveness (sometimes even subversion) within the group. Because of the conflict and the hidden agendas within his team, Carl White's project is at risk to demolition.

Misguided or negative energy for the task by itself would lead to collapse of the project. Collapse is characterized by false starts and by out-of-bounds growth in a project. And Alan Lord's project is a prime candidate. Alan feels both abandoned by his management and misled by his client. So it would be easy for him to continuously redefine his project in an attempt to satisfy every potential (rather than actual) need. If he did that the project would eventually collapse of its own weight.

A project manager's goal, of course, is a balanced investment of energy that is *on the mark*. An investment on the mark leads to projects perceived as successful by the project team, by the parent organization, by the client. In the following chapters we'll see how project managers can balance energy for the task and energy for the team as they provide for the routine care and feeding of the project team. They can

- identify the interpersonal roles and skills needed to maintain and complete group action (Chapter 11);
- encourage group performance of these roles and skills (Chapter 11);
- develop missing roles and skills in other team members when possible (Chapter 11);
- supply missing roles and skills when needed (Chapter 11);
- recognize dysfunctional roles (Chapter 12);
- discourage dysfunctional roles (Chapter 12).

11

Looking for the Best

INTRODUCTION

"The previously inefficient and frequently acrimonious situation was transformed into one of highly productive teamwork" (Holt, 1983, 4).

"It was not only successful commercially and technically but it was also a very happy and friendly project. People enjoyed working on it. . . ." (Holt, 1983, p. 8).

"A good standard of behaviour was maintained and no serious disciplinary measures were necessary. Sickness and absenteeism levels were low and no serious accidents were reported." (Holt, 1983, p. 8).

Construction projects in the Teeside region were plagued with problems during the early 1970s. As one ICI spokesman said, "Teeside was not a very good place to construct at all." It certainly didn't seem to be. Many projects were completed one to three years late. And some ran as much as 100 percent over budget.

When ICI undertook the construction of a Terephthalic acid plant (T-8) in the Teeside region in 1976, many people were skeptical. But the project manager firmly resolved that this project would be different. He studied previous projects carefully—technical teams had been of consistently high calibre. But previous team leaders had functioned primarily as senior technical people. He decided to function truly as project manager.

The result? Construction of T-8 was completed only three months late. And the project cost about 10 million pounds *under* the estimated 85 million (about 12 percent under). The project manager balanced the task requirements and the human requirements so well that comments like those beginning this chapter were typical.

How can a project manager keep his team on target—balancing his investment in project tasks and his investment in the team itself? The following chapters will answer that question and highlight some projects at Aerodigm to illustrate.

In this chapter, we'll begin by answering the question, "What is project success?" Then we'll discuss some of the steps a project manager can take to assure that critical balance between task and people:

Step A: Identify the interpersonal roles and skills needed to maintain and complete group action.

Step B: Encourage group performance of these roles and skills.

Step C: Develop missing roles and skills in other team members when possible.

Step D: Supply missing roles and skills when needed.

In the next chapter, we'll discuss the remaining steps:

Step E: Recognize dysfunctional roles.

Step F: Balance them.

WHAT IS SUCCESS?

What are the three traditional criteria for project success? Jot them down here:

1. _____

2. _____

3. _____

Right. People have traditionally thought of a successful project as one that

1. is completed on time.
2. is completed within budget.
3. meets all technical specifications.

Based on their study of 650 completed projects, researchers Baker, Murphy, and Fisher developed the definition of project success that's shown below (1983, p. 670). As you read their definition, circle the traditional criteria you find.

"If the project meets the technical performance specifications and/or missions to be performed and if there is a high level of satisfaction concerning the project outcome among key people in the parent organization, key people in the client organization, key people on the project team, and key users or clientele of the project effort, the project is considered an overall success."

Which of the traditional criteria did you find? Only one: "meets technical performance specifications."

The same researchers found that seven factors together accounted for 91 percent of the variance between projects that succeeded and projects that failed (p. 682). Write a **1** by the factor you think was most important, a **2** by the factor you think was next most important, and so on until you've written a number by each of the seven factors.

_____ Adequacy of project structure and control.

_____ Internal capabilities buildup.

_____ Success criteria salience and consensus.

_____ Project uniqueness, importance, and public exposure.

_____ Absence of competitive and budgetary pressure.

_____ Absence of initial overoptimism or conceptual difficulty.

_____ Coordination and relations.

Now compare your ranking with the research findings shown below. Which factors surprise you?

1. Coordination and relations.
2. Success criteria salience and consensus.
3. Absence of initial overoptimism or conceptual difficulty.
4. Adequacy of project structure and control.
5. Absence of competitive and budgetary pressure.
6. Project uniqueness, importance, and public exposure.
7. Internal capabilities buildup.

The coordination and relations factor alone accounted for 77 percent of the variance in perceived project success. This factor was comprised of nineteen items.

Seven of these pertained to within-team characteristics: project team spirit; sense of mission; goal commitment; capability; participation in decision making; participation in major problem solving; and supportive informal relations of team members.

Three items related to the characteristics of the project manager: his or her human skills, administrative skills, and authority.

Six items pertained to the relationship of the team to others: unity between project manager and contributing department manager; unity between project manager and his superior; job security of project team; enthusiasm of the parent organization; unity between project manager and public officials; unity between project manager and client contact.

Three items were largely technical ones which can be greatly affected by human relations: realistic progress reports, adequacy of change procedures, and availability of backup strategies.

Most of these items draw on the project manager's capacity to respond to two overlapping demands: the demand to exchange information and the demand to share authority. Project managers who meet both these demands well are called gatekeepers or technological gatekeepers.

To begin with, the project manager–gatekeeper has a broader, more current information base than the nongatekeeper. He is likely to

- consult significantly more often with organizational colleagues;
- spend significantly more time in these consultations;
- rely on more people both within their own specialties and outside their specialties;
- show the only real contact outside their specialties;
- read more—especially more hard literature;
- maintain relationships outside his organization that are broader ranging and longer lasting (Allen, 1970, p. 16).

How does the project manager–gatekeeper exchange the information within his group? How does he draw information out of other members of the group? How does the information become the base for team participation in decision making and for major problem solving? The answer to all of these questions seems to lie in a highly participative leadership style that balances energy invested in the task with energy invested in the team members.

If a project manager invests in the task alone, his team may fall apart before the task is completed. Or dissonance may result in time and cost overruns. If a project manager invests in the team members alone, he may nurture a group of very low performers.

Give yourself a balance check using the T-P Questionnaire shown in Table 11-1 and the score sheet in Figure 11-1. If you feel your investment of energy is out of line, you can use behaviors like the ones we will develop in Step A to make an adjustment.

If your balance check shows that you lean in either direction, you can find some ways to bring your orientation back into alignment in the next section.

Table 11–1
T-P Leadership Questionnaire

Directions: The following items describe aspects of leadership behavior. Respond to each item according to the way you would most likely act if you were the leader of a work group. Circle whether you would most likely behave in the described way: always (A), frequently (F), occasionally (O), seldom (S), or never (N).

A F O S N   1. I would most likely act as the spokesman of the group.
A F O S N   2. I would encourage overtime work.
A F O S N   3. I would allow members complete freedom in their work.
A F O S N   4. I would encourage the use of uniform procedures.
A F O S N   5. I would permit the members to use their own judgment in solving problems.
A F O S N   6. I would stress being ahead of competing groups.
A F O S N   7. I would speak as a representative of the group.
A F O S N   8. I would needle members for greater effort.
A F O S N   9. I would try out my ideas in the group.
A F O S N   10. I would let the members do their work the way they think best.
A F O S N   11. I would be working hard for a promotion.
A F O S N   12. I would tolerate postponement and uncertainty.
A F O S N   13. I would speak for the group if there were visitors present.
A F O S N   14. I would keep the work moving at a rapid pace.
A F O S N   15. I would turn the members loose on a job and let them go to it.
A F O S N   16. I would settle conflicts when they occur in the group.
A F O S N   17. I would get swamped by details.
A F O S N   18. I would represent the group at outside meetings.
A F O S N   19. I would be reluctant to allow the members any freedom of action.
A F O S N   20. I would decide what should be done and how it should be done.
A F O S N   21. I would push for increased production.
A F O S N   22. I would let some members have authority which I could keep.
A F O S N   23. Things would usually turn out as I had predicted.
A F O S N   24. I would allow the group a high degree of initiative.
A F O S N   25. I would assign group members to particular tasks.
A F O S N   26. I would be willing to make changes.
A F O S N   27. I would ask the members to work harder.
A F O S N   28. I would trust the group members to exercise good judgment.
A F O S N   29. I would schedule the work to be done.
A F O S N   30. I would refuse to explain my actions.
A F O S N   31. I would persuade others that my ideas are to their advantage.
A F O S N   32. I would permit the group to set its own pace.
A F O S N   33. I would urge the group to beat its previous record.
A F O S N   34. I would act without consulting the group.
A F O S N   35. I would ask that group members follow standard rules and regulations.

T _____   F _____

1. Circle the item number for items 8, 12, 17, 18, 19, 30, 34, and 35.
2. Write the number 1 in front of a *circled item number* if you responded S (seldom) or N (never) to that item.
3. Also write a number 1 in front of *item numbers not circled* if you responded A (always) or F (frequently).
4. Circle the number 1's which you have written in front of the following items: 3, 5, 8, 10, 15, 18, 19, 22, 24, 26, 28, 30, 32, 34, and 35.
5. *Count the circled number 1's.*
   Record the score in the blank following the letter P at the end of the questionnaire.
6. *Count the uncircled number 1's.*
   Record this number in the blank following the letter T.

Figure 11-1
Scoresheet

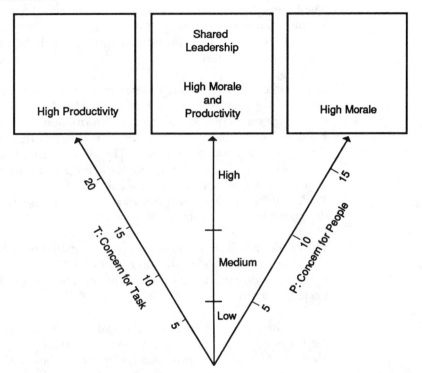

1. Mark your *T* score on the left-hand arrow above.
2. Mark your *P* score on the right-hand arrow.
3. Draw a straight line between the two points you've marked.
4. The point at which the line you've drawn cuts across the center arrow gives you a rating on "shared leadership."

Copyright 1979, Educational Research Association. Washington, D.C. Reprinted from J. William Pfeiffer & John E. Jones (Eds.), A Handbook of Structured Experiences for Human Relations Training. *Vol. I, San Diego, CA: University Associates, Inc., 1974. Used with Permission.*

◆ Step A ◆ IDENTIFY THE INTERPERSONAL ROLES AND SKILLS NEEDED TO MAINTAIN AND COMPLETE GROUP ACTION

In the spring of 1961, recently inaugurated President John Kennedy reluctantly approved U.S. support for an attack on Cuba by an exile army. The attack was ill-conceived, ill-disguised, and ill-timed. The United States expected support from antiCastro Cubans still on the island; no one gave support. The United States expected people to believe the bombers which had recently flown over Cuba were the planes of Cuban deserters; no one believed it. The United States expected Cubans to be surprised by the actual assault; no one was surprised. The April 17, 1961, Bay of Pigs fiasco is considered by most historians to be the darkest hour of John Kennedy's career.

In the fall of 1962, Kennedy ordered that all ships carrying offensive weapons to Cuba be turned back by the U. S. fleet. His action was squarely based on reliable information that Cuba was building a network of missile bases, was constructing new airfields, was uncrating Soviet jet bombers. The United States hoped that Soviet ships would turn back without a direct attack on the U. S. quarantine; the Soviet ships turned back. The October 22–28, 1962, Cuban missile crisis is considered by most historians to be the brightest hour of John Kennedy's career.

The two events were only months apart, initiated by the same president consulting with the same staff of advisors. One was a humiliating defeat; the other was an invigorating triumph. What made the difference?

The performance of Kennedy and his advisors in the first instance illustrates what can happen when some important group roles are omitted or stifled. Yale professor Irving Janis believes the same group succeeded in the second instance because Kennedy applied these remedies: he brought in outside opinion; he asked each member to be a critical evaluator; he avoided direct leadership (even absented himself from some of the discussions); and he made it clear he wanted all alternatives explored. These remedies are evidence that in the Cuban missile crisis, Kennedy performed these roles:

- he sought other opinions and information;
- he followed;
- he served as gatekeeper;
- he tested for consensus;

These are among the roles required for effective performance that are often missing from a group. We'll discuss these roles in three groups:

- roles that direct energy to the task;
- roles that direct energy to the group;
- roles that direct energy both to the task and to the group.

Roles that direct energy to the task

Betty Ashford's group overcame some initial interpersonal problems to become a highly cohesive group. But George Drexel's manager Tom Cartwright diverted some of the energy Betty directed toward the task. Betty was tempted to redefine the task or avoid it all together (thereby, avoiding Tom Cartwright) and concentrate on what feels right to her group. Instead of yielding to that temptation, however, she has seen to it that someone in her group fulfills each of these task-directed roles.

Seek other opinions and information

Within the group, Betty actively seeks opinions and information from other team members. She encourages George's contribution of ideas and information with open questions (questions that open up discussion). And she clarifies Roberta's frequent but sometimes fuzzy comments, by reflecting what Roberta has said and by asking direct questions (questions that pin down the facts).

Initiate activity

Well, Roberta is a born initiator. So in Betty's group, there's no shortage of proposed solutions, new ideas, new plans of attack, new ways to look at the information. (Betty sometimes asks the born initiator to accept responsibility during a meeting to invite proposals and plans from George).

Coordinate

Here George is unbeatable. Betty just needs to be sure he has the opportunity to point out relationships among apparently random ideas that come to the group from a variety of sources.

Summarize

Betty opens a meeting with a summary of what needs to be accomplished. She gives action summaries during the meeting. ("We have already. . . . We still need to. . . .") And she concludes each meeting with a summary of what has been accomplished, what will be covered at the next meeting, and what action items should be completed in the meantime.

Roles that direct energy to the group

Carl White's group has been beset with personality clashes. He has been tempted just to steam-roller over them in an attempt to get on with the task. But he realized that suppressing the conflicts would only make a grand explosion more likely. So he has been careful to see that someone in his group performs each of these roles.

Follow

Carl's group has two leaders: he was appointed by Walter Pruitt and Jack Thompson was appointed by himself. Carl's group has two unfollowers: Brad Thornton actively resists following or leading, and Fred Kemp passively resists them. Carl's group has only one member who by function and by disposition can be an audience, can go along with decisions of the group, can good-naturedly accept the ideas of others: Enid Schwartz. So Carl encourages Enid when she does those things. And when he can do them himself without abandoning his leadership role, he does so.

Gatekeep

Carl specifically asked for Enid's help here. When discussions get hot and heavy Enid is invaluable. She will interrupt firmly, "Wait a minute, we haven't heard from Fred yet." Or she will confidently suggest, "Since we're pushed for time, let's each limit what we say to five minutes. That way we'll be sure everyone gets to speak. I'll be timer."

Set standards

Carl's group is still having trouble agreeing on standards and specifications. Sometimes the group even strays from one of the few it has adopted. Then Carl reminds them of the standard and points out that they are steering off course.

Express group feeling

Both Carl and Enid do a lot of this —it's absolutely essential when feelings run high (or very low): "It sounds like we've all gotten frustrated to the point of anger," or "It's hard to keep pushing on when we all feel discouraged like this."

Encourage

Enid actually surpasses Carl here. She remains warm and friendly in the face of hostilities. In spite of the battles raging, she compliments worthy ideas and behavior, accepts ideas from others, and —whenever possible —expresses agreement.

Now Dan Smith's group has been relatively free of personality conflict. But he can't afford to ignore these roles, either. Dan has appropriately put a lot of energy into formal planning and formal control. But, unless he directs some energy toward his group, it would be easy for them to focus so intently on technical aspects of the task that they simply ignore one another. It will take a group effort, not merely the sum of individual efforts, to get Dan's project where he wants it to go.

Roles that direct energy toward the task and energy toward the group

Since Alan Lord's project has only loosely defined outcomes, he makes a special effort to direct energy toward the task. But he has also dealt with one interpersonal conflict after another. So it's especially important that he direct energy toward the group as well. The roles below will have double pay-offs for Alan.

Test for consensus

Like Betty, Alan frequently makes action summaries. For Alan they serve two purposes. Of course, they simply summarize —that directs energy toward the task. But they also test the water to be sure any disagreements or reservations surface before the group moves on. Sometimes Alan begins a summary with, "Are we agreed that. . .?" And sometimes he asks for opinions directly: "Laney, how do you feel about it?"

Relieve tension

Bottled up tension can block progress toward the task and splinter the team, as well. Alan carefully avoids sarcasm, but he looks for ways to get the group laughing when the tension mounts. One day he brought in an irresistible cartoon. Another day it was his $89.00 designer radish. (He and his wife were trying to grow a kitchen garden; but like many of us, they sowed more dollars than they reaped vegetables. On top of that, the precious radish was as thin as a toothpick.) And Alan is always available to listen, simply listen.

Mediate

Alan models consensus seeking for his group. He faces criticism squarely without overreacting. And he actively looks for ways to satisfy the must-haves for both parties in a conflict.

After a project manager *recognizes* these roles, what next?

◆ Step B ◆ ENCOURAGE GROUP PERFORMANCE OF THESE ROLES AND SKILLS

It would be impossible for a project manager to perform all these roles himself. And if it were possible, it wouldn't be desirable. The best of all possible worlds is to have these roles supplied by various team members. But it will take some effort on the project manager's part to evoke them. He will need to

- pay attention;
- give feedback;
- reinforce.

Pay attention

Before you read on, take a look at your watch. What time is it?

Now without looking at your watch again answer this question out loud or in writing: What kind of numerals are on the watch — Arabic or Roman? Take a look back at your watch to check. Were you right? If you were, you are unusually observant. When most people check the time, the time is all they notice. For one thing, there is no point in noticing anything else. For another thing, they are so accustomed to the face of the watch that the details have become virtually invisible.

Once a project manager has clearly defined the purpose of a meeting, announced it beforehand, and summarized it again at the beginning of the meeting, it may seem there is no point in noticing anything other than the information directly related to it. Extraneous comments, social interaction —these things just don't matter. And he may be so accustomed to these things that they become virtually invisible.

Carl has grown so accustomed to Brad Thornton's banter that he might not notice some detail —some small helpful behavior that Brad himself might try to obscure. He might not notice that Brad consistently brings new, relevant, and accurate data into the group. Whatever his motivation, Brad is thorough; and the group benefits.

And he may be so accustomed to Enid's support that her good nature and her interpersonal skill become virtually invisible to him. He may not see her routinely capable gatekeeping and encouraging.

So Carl makes noticing important roles a point on his personal agenda for each meeting. He makes a quick note when he sees one of those roles being supplied. So he is prepared to encourage its supplier.

Give feedback

What happens when you're driving at night and unexpectedly travel into a bank of heavy fog? Right. You slow down —maybe even pull over and come to a full stop. Why? Because you can't see where you're going.

Well, team members working without feedback are traveling in a fog, too. When that's the case they, too, will slow down. Progress may even come to a full stop. In fact, one summary of management research concludes that feedback is the management option with "the greatest single impact on productivity" (Cummings, Molloy, and Glen, 1975, p. 58).

Carl does his best to cut through the fog with good feedback. He gives feedback that is *specific:* "Enid, you're encouraging Brad to go ahead and test his new idea really helped break the tension." He gives feedback that is *measurable:* "Fred, I noticed you made three suggestions today that really helped us pin down our schedule. I realize you're sometimes uncomfortable speaking up, so I really appreciate it. Thanks." He gives feedback that is *goal-related:* "We had hoped to complete a list of performance requirements by the end of today's meeting. But we have finished only three of the five categories." He gives feedback that is *visual,* when possible. For example, he may ask the gatekeeper to track contributions from each member on a chart like the one shown in Figure 11-2. Then at each break team members themselves can see if they are dominating the conversation or not saying enough.

He gives feedback that is immediate. He doesn't wait a week to say, "Thanks, Brad, for coming through with that commitment from Mark last week." He thanks Brad on the spot.

Reinforce

Carl's team needs feedback —both about progress and about the lack of it. When Carl gives feedback about progress that meets the criteria of the examples above, he has accomplished two things: First, he has cut through the fog. Second, he has encouraged the repetition of the behavior that resulted in progress. In other words, he has *reinforced* the behavior.

Figure 11-2
Conversation Contribution Chart

Team Member	Number of Comments
Carl	JHT
Fred	I
Brad	JHT JHT
Enid	IIII
Jack	JHT II

Positive feedback is the least expensive and most effective reinforcer available to Carl. (Technically, it falls into the category of *social reinforcers*.) But there are others:

Gadgets

When Carl browsed through the engineering section of the local university, he came across some planning calendars designed specifically for project use. He rewarded each team member with one when they made a strategic breakthrough.

Auditory or visual signals

Carl keeps a project chart in the meeting room. He colors segments of the Critical Path as the team completes them. When the team is on schedule or ahead of it, this reinforces their progress.

Tokens

After the group met a particularly pressing deadline, Carl passed out badges that read "Winner."

Consumables

The team seemed stuck for the longest on establishing agreed-upon priorities. When they finally reached a hard-earned agreement, Carl took the whole group out to lunch.

What if some roles are missing entirely in a group? What if there's nothing to reinforce? Then a project manager can move on to the next step.

◆ Step C ◆ DEVELOP MISSING ROLES AND SKILLS IN OTHER TEAM MEMBERS WHEN POSSIBLE

Betty Ashford's team now works together amazingly well. But it has taken a lot of effort on Betty's part. In the beginning, it seemed impossible to coordinate individual information, to get a clear focus on group feeling, to ensure that everyone had a chance to speak without being pushed. Betty wanted to share the responsibility for these roles with her team. For one thing, she really wanted her team to *be* a team. For another thing, she wasn't sure she could muster the sheer brute force it would take to shoulder all the responsibility herself. Betty outlined her alternatives in order of preference.

1. Delegate
2. Rotate assignments

3. Assign individual development activity
4. Lead or assign group development
5. Provide formal training

Delegate

Responsible participation is probably the best teacher. Betty's team members certainly have the potential to supply some of the roles needed; so she will give them the responsibility. Roberta, for example, has group facilitation skills. But she got so caught up in sharing her own ideas she hadn't put much effort into seeing that everyone had a chance to contribute. Then Betty asked her to be the gatekeeper. (In this small group that role includes the function of timekeeper.) Roberta was shocked when she tracked the amount of time that her comments dominated the discussion. Then she began to see to it that Betty didn't have to shout to get a word in and that George didn't simply withdraw in self defense.

Rotate

Not only did Betty delegate some roles, she rotated them. Even though George was a natural in an organization role, Betty would sometimes ask him, before a group meeting, to be prepared to summarize group feeling if the team hit a rough spot that day.

Assign individual development activities

At first it was hard to tap George's ability to organize and coordinate information for the group as a whole. Then Betty asked him to research ways of coordinating information visually, in a way that could be shared with the group conveniently and updated easily. George developed a flow chart and a decision table that became the tools of his new role: coordinator.

Lead or assign group development activities

Betty and Roberta were both so impressed with George's flow chart and decision table, that they wanted to know more. So —to strengthen decision and coordination skills in the team as a whole —George conducted a mini-workshop on visual decision making aids.

Provide formal training

Formal training is a time consuming and costly way to develop a role. But if the need is clearly identified and the training is carefully chosen it can be a very valuable one. The group as a whole agreed they depended too much on George to coordinate information needed for decisions. So Roberta signed up for a workshop in information mapping at the local junior college to prepare her to assume more of that role.

Sometimes the potential doesn't exist within the team, because of limited capability, because of lack of disposition, because of overload. What then?

◆ Step D ◆ SUPPLY THE MISSING ROLES AND SKILLS WHEN NEEDED

At times Alan Lord has felt managing his team was like "riding off in all directions." The range and intensity of interpersonal conflicts has just seemed overwhelming. Alan explored his alternatives to provide coordination, gatekeeping, mediation, and the expression of group feeling. He could

1. Borrow a person to supply a role
2. Hire an outside consultant to supply a role
3. Hire a new person onto the team
4. Supply the role himself

Borrow a person to supply a role

When team meetings continued to be hot and heavy for a while, Alan called on the human resource department. They provided a kind of guest facilitator for a few meetings to help see to it that everyone shared information and feelings.

Hire an outside consultant to supply a role

Alan had his hands full dealing with dissension in the chain of command. When a team disagreement called for some real mediation, Alan simply felt overwhelmed. He had the skills, all right. But at that particular time one more thing was one thing too many. So he hired a consultant in conflict resolution to help.

Hire a new person onto the team

To tip the scales in his direction, Alan is looking for a person with good facilitation skills to help coordinate. He may not go outside the company; he's looking carefully around Aerodigm first. But if he needs to, he'll make facilitation skills a must in the new engineering position he's filling. And as soon as that position is filled, he'll assign the new person to this project.

Do it himself

Alan could do with fewer demands on himself personally. But he has assumed responsibility for expressing group feeling from the very beginning. And —with help in these other roles —he can continue to do so.

SUMMARY

Project success demands that the manager respond capably to two overlapping demands: the demand to exchange information and the demand to share authority. How can he generate the needed exchange of information? How can he make this information the basis for team participation and for major problem solving? He can take these steps.

Step A. Identify the interpersonal skills and roles needed to maintain and complete group action

To keep his team on balance, the project manager must recognize which roles direct energy to the task, which roles direct energy to the team, and which roles do both.

Step B. Encourage group performance of these roles and skills

To foster the performance of these roles within his group, the project manager can pay close attention to the behavior of team members, give feedback about how well the team is supplying needed roles, and reinforce the behaviors that contribute to them.

Step C. Develop missing roles and skills in other team members when possible

Sometimes the project manager may simply delegate the role to a team member with potential. Other times an individual or group development activity will provide the capability. Rotating assignments or formal training are other options.

Step D. Supply the missing roles and skills when needed

If team members have limited capacity, if they lack the necessary disposition, or if they are overloaded, the project manager may need to (1) borrow a person to supply a role; (2) hire an outside consultant to supply a role; (3) hire a new person on to the team; or (4) supply the needed role himself.

Reviewing Team Effort

On the following chart, check the adjectives you think describe the way key people feel about your project.

	Very Satisfied	Satisfied	Dissatisfied
Key people in the parent organization	_____	_____	_____
Key people on the project team	_____	_____	_____
Key people in the client organization as a whole	_____	_____	_____
Key users within the client organization	_____	_____	_____

Now rate your project on the aspects of coordination and relations (1 = we're doing very well, 5 = we're doing very poorly):

_____ project team spirit

_____ project team sense of mission

_____ project team goal commitment

_____ project team capability

_____ project manager's administrative skills

_____ unity between project manager and contributing department managers

_____ job security of the project team

_____ project team participation in decision making

_____ project team participation in major problem solving

_____ supportive internal team relations

_____ project manager's human skills

_____ project manager's authority

_____ unity between project manager and his own manager

_____ enthusiasm of parent organization

_____ unity between project manager and public officials

_____ unity between project manager and client contact

_____ realistic progress reports

_____ availability of backup strategies

Now check every characteristic of a gatekeeper you feel applies to you.

_____ I consult significantly more often with organizational colleagues.

_____ I spend significantly more time in these consultations.

_____ I rely on more people both within my own specialty and outside their specialty.

_____ I show the only real contact outside my own specialty.

_____ I read more—especially more hard literature.

_____ I maintain relationships outside my organization that are broader ranging and longer lasting.

Identifying Needed Roles

Put a check by the roles you feel are already well-supplied in your team. Circle the ones that still need to be supplied.

1. Roles that direct energy to the task
   —Seek other opinions and information
   —Initiate activity
   —Coordinate
   —Summarize

2. Roles that direct energy to the group
   —Follow
   —Gatekeep
   —Set standards
   —Express group feeling
   —Encourage

3. Roles that direct energy toward the task and toward the group
   —Test for consensus
   —Relieve tension
   —Mediate

Encouraging Performance

What team members are supplying the roles you checked above? How will you reinforce their behavior (social reinforcers, gadgets, signals, tokens, consumables)?

Role	Supplier	Reinforcement You Can Provide

Developing Missing Roles

Which roles that you circled can you develop in team members (delegate, assign individual development activity, lead or assign group development activity, rotate assignments, provide formal training)?

Role   Supplier   How You Will Develop Role

_____   _____   _____

  _____

  _____

_____   _____   _____

  _____

  _____

_____   _____   _____

  _____

  _____

_____   _____   _____

  _____

  _____

Supplying Missing Roles

Which roles circled must you supply in some other way? How will you do it
(borrow a person, hire an outside consultant, hire a new person on to the
team, supply the role yourself)?

Role   How You Will Supply It

_____   _____

                   _____

_____   _____

                   _____

_____   _____

                   _____

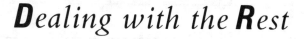

12

Dealing with the **R**est

INTRODUCTION

In the 1948 novel No Highway, *protagonist Theodore Honey warned of fatigue failure in his company's new transAtlantic aircraft, the Reindeer. His warnings fell on deaf ears. True, fatigue failures had characterized the introduction of other forms of transportation (such as the railroads). But fatigue failures wouldn't be a problem in this case. No need for additional testing, no need for extensive inspections here.*

A Reindeer crash in Canada was quickly written off to pilot error. Desperate, Honey tampered with the landing gear of another Reindeer to keep it from taking off. Finally, someone paid attention and ordered a reexamination of the Canadian wreckage. What did they find? Telltale signs of fatigue.

In 1953 the de Havilland Comet "flew off the drawing board." The Comet's designers had been ultraconservative. They had overdesigned the first commercial jet aircraft. True, its highly pressurized cabin was an important new structure. But there would be no fatigue problems in this case. No need, even, for a prototype.

On May 2, 1953, a de Havilland Comet was destroyed on takeoff from a Calcutta airport. The incident was written off to either the weather or to pilot error. On January 10, 1954, a Comet exploded on takeoff from Rome. The weather was mild and clear. But there were no strong clues pointing to another cause. On April 8, 1954, another Comet exploded on takeoff from Rome. The remains fell into waters too deep for recovery. So the search for remains from the previous explosion was renewed. Close examination of newly recovered fragments showed undeniable evidence of fatigue failure in the cabin structure. (Petroski, 1986,
pp. 176–188)

Nevil Shute, author of *No Highway* (and later of *On the Beach*), added this author's note in addition to the usual disclaimer:

"This book is a work of fiction. None of the characters are drawn from real persons. The Reindeer aircraft in my story is not based on any particular commercial aircraft, nor do the troubles from which it suffered refer to any actual events. . . ."

Reindeer? *Flying* Reindeer? Dancer, Prancer, *Comet,* Blitzen? As Nevil Norway, Shute had worked for de Havilland fresh out of Oxford as a stress calculator. He had known the head of the structural department at Farnborough—the site of pioneer work on metal fatigue during the 1940s.

There's no way of knowing if Shute, like his fictional hero, had warned about fatigue failure. There's no way of knowing if he, like his fictional hero, had been ignored by deaf ears. But we do know that in many project failures a deaf ear was turned to someone who had critical information to share—information not accepted (perhaps not even really heard) until the project's post mortem.

A project failure can yield breakthrough data for future projects. But the cost of the breakthrough is painfully high. Better if we could avoid forensic project management or—at worst—reserve it for post mortems of *other* people's projects, not our own. Yet project success will require not only that we visualize a model of success, but also that we see signs of failure and deal with them before it is too late.

We developed an interpersonal model for success in the last chapter. In this chapter we will identify warning signs of failure. A kind of interpersonal radar can help.

Figure 12–1
Project Management Radar

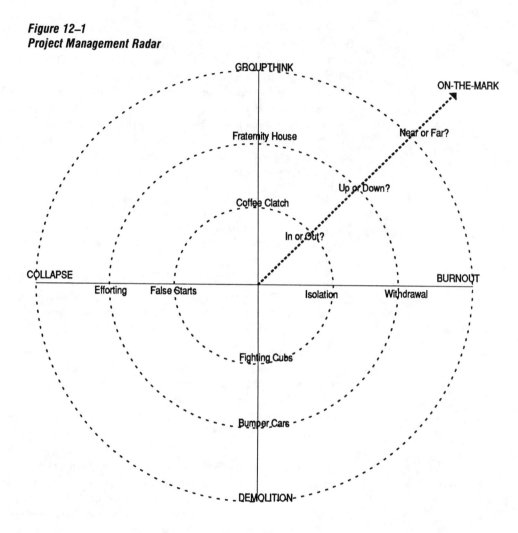

The vector in Figure 12-1 shows a project on the mark. A project on the mark, like the Cuban missile crisis, balances positive energy directed toward the team with positive energy directed toward the task.

The axes in Figure 10-1 chart signs of failure.

- Groupthink results from an excess of positive energy directed toward the team without the balance of positive energy for the task.
- Burnout results from an excess of positive energy directed toward the task without the balance of positive energy for the team.

- Demolition results from an excess of negative energy directed toward the team.
- Collapse results from an excess of negative energy directed toward the task.

As we investigate each axis, we will see how a project manager can take the remaining steps to care for and feed his project team:

Step E: Recognize dysfunctional roles. (We'll describe the signs, look at examples, and explore causes.)

Step F: Balance dysfunctional roles. (We'll develop antidotes.)

In this chapter, our discussion of STEPS E and F will be incorporated into discussions of the four axes. (Don't be thrown off—in earlier chapters, we organized around the steps themselves.) But, as before, we'll highlight some projects at Aerodigm as we go.

GROUPTHINK
The signs

Groupthink (a term coined by Yale professor Irving Janis) is a highly cohesive state of striving for consensus. Groupthink results from excess positive energy directed toward the group without a balance of energy directed toward the task. Characterized by "It's us against the world" lines of thinking, it can lead to bad decisions, to reckless behavior. In fact, Janis attributes a number of historical fiascoes to groupthink: U. S. failure to shore up defense of Pearl Harbor; Truman's decision to cross the 38th Parallel in Korea; the Kennedy administration's decisions about the Bay of Pigs.

"Since Cartwright is such a nuisance, let's just leave him out of it. Even if he doesn't like it, how can he hurt us?"

"None of those people in the front office have any idea what's going on in the Real World, anyway!"

"We'd have gotten it in on time if Walter Pruitt just hadn't abandoned us."

"If it weren't right, we wouldn't feel so good about it."

These comments by Betty Ashford's team members illustrate four of the warnings Professor Janis spells out: the illusion of invulnerability (willingness to take excessive risk); shared stereotypes, rationalization, and the illusion of morality. There are two others. Selfcensorship is the suppression of information by the informed person himself—the refusal (out of fondness, not out of fear) to tell the boss something he doesn't want to hear. Mindguarding is the suppression of information for the same reason by a gatekeeper—someone who can block the informed person from reaching the boss.

At first, the comments from Betty's team members seemed lighter—like the gossip you'd expect at a coffee klatch. However, instead of fading as the group matured, the remarks became harsher—like some of the caustic criticism of nonmembers you'd hear in a fraternity house. Then Betty came across this warning in a project management text, and her vague concerns crystallized.

"When the search for scapegoats begins in earnest, and dominates activity, one can be certain that the project is dead. The principal players are merely arguing over its bones" (Gilbreath, 1986, p. 16).

The antidotes

Betty recognized the risk of her group's becoming *too* cohesive—cohesive to the point of disregarding outsiders. She didn't want to wait until they were arguing over the bones of her project. She made some in-flight course corrections.

- She sought other opinions and information. Alan Lord and Betty both report to Walter Pruitt. Both have had project problems as a result of Walter's insistence on being "left out of it." Alan has apparently had some recent successes in dealing with Walter. So Betty asked Alan to share some ideas with her group.
- She has followed, rather than led, at some group meetings. In several situations, Betty's loyal group has seen her as the victim of outsiders—specifically Walter Pruitt and Tom Cartwright. These situations actually became rallying points. (Like "Remember the Maine!") Perhaps part of the problem was too much attention focused on Betty herself. So she rotated leadership—asked Roberta and George each to lead a project meeting. And on one occasion she asked Roberta and George to brainstorm as a subgroup in her absence.
- She has concentrated on the roles of gatekeeping and testing for consensus. Even when Betty has remained meeting leader, she has made it clear that she wanted all alternatives explored. She has been careful to get all opinions on the table and has asked each team member to be a critical evaluator of the group's decisions.

BURNOUT
The signs

Herbert Freudenberger (1980, p. 17) coined the term burnout and defined it this way: "To deplete oneself. To exhaust one's physical and mental resources. To wear oneself out by excessively striving to reach some unrealistic expectation imposed by one's self or by the values of society." Burnout is an outcome of intense individual effort toward the task without team support. The project may fail because it requires the 2 + 2 = 5 effect of a team, not merely the sum of individual efforts. On the other hand, the task may get done, but the welfare of individual team members is likely to be sacrificed in the process.

The beleaguered Surveyor II program, for example, was handicapped by lack of teamwork and lack of senior management involvement. Surveyor II was expected, like its predecessor, to take photographs of and collect data from the moon. But it lost contact with the earth five and a half hours before its predicted lunar landing.

Then there's the tragic story of Roger Berman. Berman's job became more and more difficult for him. It required more and more evening and weekend hours of him. It satisfied him less and less. It allowed him less and less to be himself. Berman asked for help but he got none. He asked for a lightened workload, he asked for early retirement. His company made promises but gave no relief. As if trying to satisfy an insatiable god, Berman worked harder and harder. Until January 31, 1979. Then he went home early and killed himself. Mrs. Berman charged his company with murder (Rice, 1981, p. 78).

Dan Smith's project has appropriately relied heavily on formal planning and formal controls. Dan didn't expect any interpersonal squabbles within the team and he hasn't seen any. He was prepared for some hassles with top management, but even those haven't materialized.

Dan has enjoyed the absence of interpersonal squabbles. But the absence of almost all interpersonal activity has begun to trouble him: What began as isolation with one team member has now developed into withdrawal. He seems angry all the time, but doesn't express anger. He listens stonily to Dan's suggestions, but doesn't follow them. Another team member seems chronically exhausted. She has remarked about her job, "Well, now that I finally have what I wanted, I realize I don't want it anymore." Yet she continues to overdo the work until she can't do it at all—until she seems immobilized by either fatigue or discouragement.

The antidotes

In *When All You Ever Wanted Isn't Enough* Harold Kushner recalls an interview with an eighty-five-year-old woman:

"If I had it to do over. . . . If I had my life to live over, I would dare to make more mistakes next time. I would relax. I would be sillier, I would take fewer things seriously. I would eat more ice cream and less beans. I would perhaps have more actual troubles but fewer imaginary ones. You see, I'm one of those people who have lived seriously and sanely hour after hour, day after day, I've been one of those persons who never went any place without a thermometer, a hot water bottle, a raincoat, and a parachute. If I had it to do again, I'd travel lighter."

Dan recognized the need to help his group "travel lighter." Like Betty, he sought other opinions and information. Like Betty, he paid attention to his role as gatekeeper. In addition

- he coordinated efforts;
- he expressed group feeling;
- he encouraged;
- he relieved tension.

Dan coordinated group efforts. He frequently referred to the big picture and pointed out ways that individual aspects of the project were fitting together.

"Eleanor, Ken has covered some territory in his research that would be good background for this part of the project. Touch base with him and let me know what you find out. I'm enjoying seeing this all come together."

"Great, Jack. This is just what Ken needs to get around that vibration problem. Please talk with him this morning and then get back with me after lunch."

He summarized group feeling, as well as facts, at every project meeting.

"The individual facets of this job are really absorbing. I know you feel I've taken you away from important work to get together like this. You'd rather be back in your shops."

"I realize it's frustrating to spend time hashing over a detail like this."

Both to individuals and to the group as a whole, Dan gives encouragement.

"Ken, I know it's difficult to work with all this time pressure. But you're handling it well. You've eliminated over half the time slippage this week."

"We're back on schedule now. And it looks like we may come in a little under the money."

And he made an extra effort to relieve tension. He tried his best to give the group some ice cream along with the beans. He arranged some sort of celebration each time the group completed a critical activity: once he brought some homemade bread to share, once he divided leftover Halloween candy. He made some lighthearted note of many little-recognized historic days: the anniversary of the first recorded use of a fork, the anniversary of the Battle of Hastings, the day a now-popular soft drink was introduced as an "esteemed Brain Tonic and Intellectual Beverage." He gave individual team members a safety valve when they need one: "Come on, Eleanor, time for a coffee break. I'm buying."

DEMOLITION
The signs

January 13, 1982. Four times Air Florida copilot Roger Pettit warned the pilot conditions were not right for takeoff. He warned about ice and snow on the plane—about instrument readings that showed engine trouble. But within seconds the plane took off with a groan, then slammed into Washington's 14th Street bridge and plunged into the Potomac. Seventy-four people died (Burrows, 1982, pp. 43-47).

Summer 1981. A senior lender with Continental Illinois (then ranked first among lenders to U.S. corporations) warned an executive vice-president of problems with the Penn Square of Oklahoma account. The vice-president sent three auditing teams to Penn Square between Summer 1981 and January 1982. All three teams confirmed the serious problems identified by the senior lender. But the bank continued to buy loans from Penn Square. On July 5, 1982, Penn Square Bank of Oklahoma failed. By September Continental had written off $286 million in bad loans and leases. Within a year the value of its holdings dropped 40 percent (Ehrbar, 1983).

In situations like these, critical information is either distorted, lost, or ignored. Sometimes the informed person is ignored in stony silence like Theodore Honey in *No Highway*. Sometimes the informed person is discredited with a direct attack like the copilot who was told by his captain, "I'll do what I want. You just look out the damn window" (Burrows, 1982). There is energy directed at the team in these cases; but the energy is destructive. Ultimately the result is demolition of the project or the team or both. The project—sometimes literally—explodes.

A team headed for groupthink places blame without. A team headed for demolition places it within. In early stages, the team resembles a den of fighting cubs. As the group matures and the fighting gets rougher, team members feel the knock as if they were riding in bumper cars. More and more, group interaction is characterized by signs of hostility: sarcasm, absence of response, temper explosions, gross overstatement, deliberate distortion of information, and catastrophizing. (Catastrophizing is the unrealistic description of situations as matters of life or death.)

Carl White's group has been a good candidate for demolition as these comments at a project meeting illustrate.

"If you ask me, this whole project has been a disaster from the very beginning."

"You're going about that all wrong."

"Stop trying to stall us again with more of your whining."

Antidotes

Like Dan, Carl offered encouragement and helped relieve tension. In addition

- he mediated;
- he set standards.

When Carl mediated ongoing discussions in his group, he used many of the same techniques he had used in handling specific conflicts. He listened carefully and summarized what he heard from each group member. Then he summarized the combined result:

"Sounds like you agree that we need standards to cover the situations we have listed on the board. But you don't agree on the specific limits that we can accept on several items."

When the group agreed his summary was accurate, he asked questions that opened further discussion about what the standards needed to accomplish. By focusing attention on what needed to be accomplished, Carl helped team members loosen their holds on some premature positions over methods.

"What specific problems would good standards have prevented in the past?"

"What maximum limit on this standard would have prevented that problem?"

"What potential problems do we want these standards to prevent?"

"What maximum limit on this standard would prevent that problem?"

"What result would this standard need to get in order for you to feel it is a good one?"

Throughout group discussions, Carl looked for win-win alternatives. He made sure any hidden losses got out in the open:

"What problems would this standard as it is written now cause your group, Enid?"

And Carl referred often to standards. Of course every group has standards for the project itself. But because of the high conflict potential in Carl's team, his group developed some standards for interpersonal behavior as well. These standards answered questions such as:

- How will we routinely share information at group meetings?
- What group responsibilities will we rotate? How?
- What group responsibilities will we permanently assign? To whom?
- How will we limit discussions?
- How will we settle disagreements?
- How will we cool off a disagreement that has gotten out of hand?
- What will be the consequences for lateness or absence from a meeting?

COLLAPSE
The signs

Bell Labs is universally considered a premier research and development organization. And the Lab's role in recovery from a 1969 service crisis at New York Telephone is an excellent example of a project on the mark. But many analysts consider the Lab's uninvolvement in field problems with the Electronic Switching System to be a critical contributor to the crisis. A 1955 commitment to Electronic Switching Stations predicted a target date of 1959 and a cost of $45 million for development. In fact, it was 1969 before Electronic Switching Stations were in widespread use and development costs had surpassed $500 million (Gibson, 1981, p. 108). There were undeniable signs of collapse by 1960. However, as one analyst put it, ". . . the project had to go forward; by this time the investment was too great to be sacrificed . . ."(Brooks, 1975, p. 278).

It was the summer of 1969 when a crisis at New York Telephone revealed a serious operating problem: old switching systems overloaded gradually giving warning signals all along; an overloaded ESS went out virtually all at once. That's what happened when the PLaza 8 exchange failed putting 10,400 phones out of service several weeks for the major part of the business day (Brooks, 1975, pp. 290–291).

In a project headed for Collapse, much energy is directed toward the task. But the energy is negative or misdirected. Signs that a project may collapse of its own weight include:

- False starts. The feedback loop seems the size of a pinhead. A team barely gets moving before they realize they have to start over again.
- "Efforting." If work is an input of energy that generates an increased output; efforting is an input of energy that produce no output at all. The effort seems to be disappearing down a sink hole.
- Migrant objectives. The project manager ignores the change control process, so the client shifts objectives frequently. And the project team itself—perhaps in self defense—shifts. Objectives become hedges: to lower the capacity and to level the cash flow.
- Out of bounds growth of a project. Five years grows to fifteen. A budget of $250,000 grows to $2.5 million. The project's reputation is predominantly for time and budget overruns, not for technical progress.

- Abandonment. Abandonment *by* a client or *by* management can be a cause or a symptom of collapse. Clients don't return phone calls. Top managers—previously on a first name basis—no longer speak to a team member passing in the hall. Abandonment *of* a client is likely to result in collapse. Team members are a better judge of what's good for a client than the client himself. Besides, the team already knows what the client wants, why keep in touch?

Early in his project, Alan saw the potential for its collapse. Every time Alan submitted a tentative plan to his client, Mark Johnson, he would hear, "Well, that's not really what we need." No other information forthcoming, Alan felt he could be forever going back to the drawing board. Each time he went back, he felt he was fruitlessly pouring more and more energy down a bottomless pit.

Since Alan undertook the project, Johnson's definition of the problem has changed again and again. If Alan continued to let Johnson's objectives migrate accordingly, project time and cost would skyrocket. As if that weren't enough, Johnson blocked Alan's access to key people in production. Alan just wasn't able to maintain contact with people whose input he needed.

Alan also felt abandoned by his own management. Over and over, when he approached his supervisor, Walter Pruitt, the message was the same: "Leave me out of it."

The antidotes

The Bell System's response to the service crisis was spectacular. Key people shared information, coordinated efforts, diagnosed problems, set new standards, and mediated. The beginning of the end of the crisis was marked by New York Telephone's William Sharwell's publicly acknowledging that the crisis was indeed a crisis, not just an episode (Brooks, p. 292). Then Sharwell proceeded to muster resources from Western Electric, Bell Labs, and AT&T. At Bell Labs, management engineered a restructuring of priorities and an overhaul of communication patterns with the operating companies.

Alan used some similar strategies to head off the collapse of his project.

- Alan shared information. He let both Walter Pruitt and Mark Johnson know what they were contributing to project problems and how they could contribute to solutions.

- He did plenty of gatekeeping. Gatekeeping has been a major role of each of our project managers. In Alan's case, he needed as much gatekeeping between his team and the rest of the company as he needed within the team.
- Alan did his best to coordinate. Coordination with his client and with his own management were as important as coordination within his own team.
- Alan diagnosed the false starts and the efforting. He identified the support he needed to make progress.
- Alan helped engineer standards. He helped establish some standard for interaction between the team and the rest of the organization as well as within the project team. These standards included a change control procedure which he invoked often in his dealings with Mark Johnson. His team developed technical performance standards for the project. When objectives drifted, Alan used the performance standards to anchor them.
- Alan mediated. Like Carl, Alan mediated differences within his team. In addition, his success would require mediation between his client and his own management. He listened carefully, then summarized both feeling and fact. He asked questions to open discussion and shifted people's attention from methods to outcomes. He uncovered the hidden costs of the project, and he referred often to standards.

SUMMARY

A project on target balances positive energy directed toward the team with positive energy directed toward the task. A project manager must keep his eye on a model of success and at the same time watch for the early signs of project failure. He must take these steps:

Step E: Recognize dysfunctional roles that can divert his project toward groupthink, burnout, demolition, or collapse.

Step F: Balance dysfunctional roles by supplying those roles needed to get the project back on target.

Table 12-1 profiles the axes on project radar: the early signs of potential failure and the antidotes a project manager can use.

Table 12–1
Description of Axes on Project Radar

DIRECTION	GROUPTHINK Highly cohesive state of striving for consensus.	BURNOUT Isolation with depletion of physical and mental resources to attain a goal.	DEMOLITION The result of escalating infighting.	COLLAPSE Out of bounds project behavior.
DANGER	Bad technical decisions.	Project failure (from lack of team effort) or the sacrifice of individual team members.	"Explosion" of the team or the project or both.	Collapse of project from its own weight.
SYMPTOMS	Illusion of invulnerability Shared stereotypes Rationalization Illusion of morality Self censorship Mind guarding	Isolation Withdrawal Exhaustion	Blaming within Sarcasm Absence of response Temper explosions Gross overstatement Distortion of information Catastrophizing	False Starts "Efforting" Migrant objectives Out of bounds growth Abandonment
BENCHMARKS	Coffee Klatch Fraternity House	Isolation Withdrawal	Fighting Cubs Bumper Cars	False Starts "Efforting"
ANTIDOTES	Gatekeep. Seek other opinions and information. Follow. Test for consensus.	Gatekeep. Coordinate. Express group feeling. Encourage. Relieve tension.	Encourage. Relieve tension. Mediate. Set standards	Gatekeep. Share information. Coordinate. Diagnose. Set standards. Mediate.

Recognizing and Balancing Dysfunctional Roles

On the following chart, circle the early symptoms of potential failure you have seen in your project.

Symptoms of Failure and Their Antidotes

DIRECTION	GROUPTHINK Highly cohesive state of striving for consensus.	BURNOUT Isolation with depletion of physical and mental resources to attain a goal.	DEMOLITION The result of escalating infighting.	COLLAPSE Out of bounds project behavior.
SYMPTOMS	Illusion of Invulnerability Shared stereotypes Rationalization Illusion of morality Self censorship Mind guarding	Isolation Withdrawal Exhaustion	Blaming within Sarcasm Absence of response Temper explosions Gross overstatement Distortion of information Catastrophizing	False Starts "Efforting" Migrant objectives Out of bounds growth Abandonment
ANTIDOTES	Gatekeep. Seek other opinions and information. Follow. Test for consensus.	Gatekeep. Coordinate. Express group feeling. Encourage. Relieve tension.	Encourage. Relieve tension. Mediate. Set standards.	Gatekeep. Share information. Coordinate. Diagnose. Set standards. Mediate.

Next, use the same chart to identify those roles you can use to get your project back on target.

Now, note specific actions you will take to activate the roles you identified.

Gatekeep. _____

_____

_____

_____

Seek other opinions and information. _____

_____

_____

_____

Follow. _____

_____

_____

_____

Test for consensus. _____

_____

_____

_____

Coordinate. _____

_____

_____

_____

Express group feeling. _____

_____

_____

_____

Encourage. _____

_____

_____

_____

Relieve tension. _____

_____

_____

_____

Mediate. _____

_____

_____

_____

Set standards. _____

_____

_____

_____

Share information. _____

_____

_____

_____

Diagnose. _____

_____

_____

_____

13

Getting Back to Real Life

We'll say it one more time: real life is the hard part. Putting this procedure to work will take time and effort on your part. And you're probably already working under overload.

The most difficult thing will be remembering—when you're under fire—what to try when. This review chapter can help. It's more than a review, actually, it's a checklist. You can use it in your planning time each day to review the most relevant part of the procedure for the current stage of your project. You can (1) take stock of where you are and (2) plan steps of the procedure into your daily task list.

And don't forget: throughout the process picture yourself succeeding!

◆Key I◆ PLAN THE INTERACTION (pp. 27–29)

◆Step A◆ IDENTIFY THE MANAGEMENT TOOLS THAT ARE LIKELY TO CONTRIBUTE MOST TO PROJECT SUCCESS (pp. 29–57)

Select management tools based on team's experience with project technology and the extent of agreement on project outcomes (pp. 30–34).
Use the tool of external integration (pp. 34–43).

1. Select clients as project team members (pp. 36–37). Look for
   - Someone who is technically competent;
   - Someone who is an opinion leader;
   - Someone who has worked with you or with other team members before.
     If this isn't possible, look for someone who has a good track record on interdepartmental projects.
2. Place clients in key positions on project teams (pp. 37–38).
   - Assign specific roles for each meeting and rotate them: historian, conscience, gatekeeper, time keeper.
   - Let client know role assignment ahead of time.
   - Give client opportunity to represent the team publicly.
3. Involve clients in key decisions such as approval of specifications and of key action dates (pp. 38–40).
   - Distribute agenda.
   - Distribute summary.
4. Clearly define areas of client responsibility (like management of a change control process, education about a new system installation of the system (pp. 40–41).
   - Draft list of client responsibilities.
   - Revise list for project agreement.
   - Establish change control procedure.
5. Communicate formally with other members of the client group (p. 41).
   - Establish contact with key users.
   - Establish contact with every member of the client group who has a responsibility listed in the revised project agreement.

6. Communicate systematically with key people in your organization as a whole—as with progress reports to a corporate steering committee (pp. 41–43).
   - Keep in touch with the mainstream.
   - When you talk to management always be on time, always have a notebook and pen, always have an executive summary on the tip of your tongue, get to the point quickly, never allow a part of the truth to paint an inaccurate picture, never drop a bomb.

Use the tool of internal integration (pp. 48–57).

1. Select experienced technical people to the project team (pp. 50–51).
2. Select team members who have worked together before. If that's not possible look for people with good track records on interdepartmental projects (pp. 51–52).
   - Be explicit about specific assignments.
   - Be explicit about group roles.
3. Select a compatible project manager (or *be* compatible) (pp. 53–54).
   - Be there.
   - Listen.
   - Respond with respect.
4. Communicate within the team (pp. 54–56).
   - Rotate roles.
   - Distribute an agenda.
   - Provide meeting summaries.
   - Meet at the right intervals.
   - Meet on the right day and at the right time.
   - Meet at the right location.
   - Seek consensus.
   - Give support.
   - Be honest but not negative.
5. Involve team members in setting goals and deadlines (p. 56).
   - Provide agenda that includes action items and decisions you expect to surface.
   - Provide summary including action items and decisions agreed upon.
6. Get outside technical assistance (p. 56) if
   - things are not going well at all;
   - things are going too well.

✦ Step B ✦ | VISUALIZE KEY PEOPLE AND THEIR LOCATION ACROSS BOUNDARIES IN THE ORGANIZATION (pp. 61–67)

1. List key people (p. 64). Include
   - the decision maker;
   - the opinion leader;
   - the gatekeeper;
   - the client;
   - team members;
   - big brothers;
   - little brothers.
2. Identify the technology of each person (pp. 63, 65).
3. Rank order the technology by degree of abstractness (pp. 63, 66).
4. Place each key person on an organizational pyramid scaled to visualize the depth and the span of the project (pp. 67).

✦ Step C ✦ | ANALYZE CONFLICTING PRESSURES IN THE ORGANIZATION AND THE IMPACT THE PROJECT (OR AN IDEA) WILL HAVE ON THEM (pp. 67–71)

1. Know what each key person will gain.
2. Know what each key person will lose.

✦ Step D ✦ | BUILD KEY ELEMENTS INTO A NEGOTIATION PLAN (pp. 72–73)

Plan ways you can

1. collaborate in setting goals;
2. consult before a critical event to set parameters;
3. enlist moral support;
4. secure the autonomy for each team member to do what needs to be done;
5. reinforce each person's effort to do what you want.

◆ Step E ◆

ORGANIZE WHAT YOU KNOW ABOUT KEY PEOPLE AND THE INTERACTION BETWEEN THEM TO GET AN EDGE ON PERSONALITY CONFLICT (pp. 72, 74)

Make notes on each person's

1. personal style;
2. relationship with you;
3. relationship with other key people;
4. pressures (job-related and other) to accept your idea;
5. pressures (job-related and other) to resist your idea.

◆ Step F ◆

BUILD A WIN-WIN PRESENTATION INTO YOUR NEGOTIATION STYLE (pp. 72, 75–79)

1. Incorporate a person's strongest job-related reason to resist into an empathy statement.
2. Select a connecting word to tell your listener you're changing directions.
3. Incorporate a person's strongest job-related reason to accept your idea in a statement of the problem as you see it.
4. Select a connecting word to tell your listener there's more to come.
5. Accommodate major nonjob-related pressures in the course of action you recommend.

◆ **Key II** ◆   TAKE A CLOSER LOOK AT HOW PROJECT SUCCESS CAN BE AFFECTED BY PERSONAL STYLES (pp. 98–114)

◆ **Step A** ◆   EXAMINE NEW ROLES AND RELATIONSHIPS (pp. 102–104)

1. How will relationships be affected by your new role to get work done through other people?
2. How will relationships be affected by your responsibility to develop team members?
3. How will relationships be affected by your responsibility to set and track priorities?
4. How will relationships be affected by your need to market your project?
5. How will relationships be affected by your need for routine contact with higher management and with your client?

◆ **Step B** ◆   ASSESS THE AMOUNT OF CONTROL YOU EXPECT IN GENERAL (pp. 104–108)

1. If possible, respond to the Rotter Scale (pp. 104–105).
2. Analyze your lifeline (pp. 105–108).

◆ **Step C** ◆   STUDY YOUR BEHAVIOR IN SPECIFIC RELATIONSHIPS (pp. 108–111)

Answer these questions about your relationships with other key people. If possible, get help from the FIRO-B (p. 108).

1. Around which people do you feel crowded (pp. 108–109)?
2. Around which people do you feel left out (p. 109)?
3. Around which people do you feel pushed (pp. 109–110)?
4. Around which people do you feel directionless (p. 110)?
5. Around which people do you feel smothered (pp. 110–111)?
6. Around which people do you feel rejected (p. 111)?

◆ **Step D** ◆ CHOOSE THE BEST COURSE OF ACTION (pp. 112–114)

1. If the difference between what you want and what you're getting doesn't matter, just live and let live (p. 112).
2. If you answer these questions "yes," then modify your own behavior (pp. 112–113).
   - Is it clear that your own behavior is out of line?
   - Is the cost of changing your own behavior small while the cost to the other person of changing his behavior is great?
   - Is the other person unable to change?
3. If you're not clear what to do about a difference, then give and get feedback about it (p. 113).
4. If you answer these three questions "yes," then negotiate for a change in the other person's behavior (pp. 113–114).
   - Does the behavior matter?
   - Would a change in your behavior alone harm the project?
   - Is at least part of the solution clear?

◆ Key III ◆   HANDLE THE CONFLICT (pp. 122–182)

◆ Step A ◆   EXPECT CONFLICT AND PLAN AHEAD HOW TO DEAL WITH IT (pp. 124–130)

Compare your expectations about project conflict with the experiences and opinions of other project managers.

1. Check conflict rankings in survey for the current phase of your project.
2. Rank the sources of conflict as you see them.
3. Compare your rankings with survey rankings.
4. If your rankings differ drastically from the survey, get a second opinion.
5. Identify those situations that may be personality conflicts in disguise.

Plan ahead how to deal with it (pp. 130–134).

1. Develop a mental framework that allows you to view conflict nonjudgmentally (pp. 130–132).
   - Identify situations that center around the question "Am I in or out?"
   - Identify situations that center around the question "Am I up or down?"
   - Identify situations that center around the question "Am I near or far?"
2. Analyze key people in your market (pp. 132–133). Make notes on each person's
   - personal style;
   - relationship with you;
   - relationship with other people;
   - pressures (job-related and other) to accept your idea;
   - pressures (job-related and other) to resist your idea.
3. Write a tentative "script" to approach each key person (pp. 132, 134).
   - Incorporate a person's strongest job-related reason to resist in an empathy statement.
   - Select a connecting word to tell your listener you're changing directions.

- Incorporate a person's strongest job-related reason to accept your idea in a statement of the problem as you see it.
- Select a connecting word to tell your listener there's more to come.
- Accommodate major nonjob-related pressures in the course of action you recommend.

◆ Step B ◆ | HAVE YOUR OWN STRESS MANAGEMENT TECHNIQUES IN PLACE BEFORE THE PROJECT BEGINS (pp. 132, 135–138)

1. Recognize a stressful situation in time to do something about it (p. 135).
   - Identify your body's signals that you are approaching your personal Plimsoll line
   - Recognize the signals your body is giving you now.
2. Tell yourself you can handle the stressful situation calmly (pp. 136–138).
   - Talk back to the negative voices in your head.
   - Find humor when you can.
   - Work smarter.
   - Clear space in your day for relaxation and exercise.
   - Assert yourself without being insensitive to others.

◆ Step C ◆ | SERVE AS A LIGHTNING ROD (p. 148)

1. Put yourself on hold (p. 150).
   - Remain quiet. Set your own feelings, your own agenda aside.
   - Give full attention to the other person.
2. Screen out distractions (pp. 150–151).
   - Face the other person.
   - Lean toward the other person.
   - Draw close enough to the other person.
   - Maintain eye contact.
3. Give it some time. Wait 10 seconds before you speak (p. 151).
4. Respond to both the feeling content and the factual content of the situation (pp. 151–152).
   - Name without blame.

- Use statements like: "You seem to feel . . . because. . . ."
- Use statements like "When . . . I feel. . . ."

◆ Step D ◆ | EXCAVATE THE REAL ISSUES (pp. 152–160)

1. Treat the surface issue as "real" three times (maybe two is enough) (pp. 152–153).
2. After the third (or second) time, begin to excavate by saying something such as, "sounds like you feel . . . because. . . ." or by using the assertive model (pp. 153–154).
3. Use planning or other aids (like the Linear Responsibility Chart) to make conflicting issues "visible" to the other parties involved (pp. 154–160).
4. Give loads of support (p. 160).

◆ Step E ◆ | LOOK FOR WIN-WIN ALTERNATIVES (pp. 172–178)

1. Do the doable (p. 173).
2. Build on your earlier analysis (pp. 173–174). Review each person's
   - personal style
   - relationship with you;
   - relationship with other key people;
   - pressures (job-related and other) to accept your idea;
   - pressures (job-related and other) to resist your idea.
3. Use the assertive model (pp. 173, 175).
   - Incorporate a person's strongest job-related reason to resist into an empathy statement.
   - Select a connecting word to tell your listener you're changing directions.
   - Incorporate a person's strongest job-related reason to accept your idea in a statement of the problem as you see it.
   - Select a connecting word to tell your listener there's more to come.
   - Accommodate major nonjob–related pressures in the course of action you recommend.

4. Look at things right side up (pp. 173, 177).
   - Don't catastrophize.
   - Separate the person from the problem.
   - Separate the person from his own behavior.
   - Focus on outcomes instead of positions.
5. Picture things going well (pp. 177–178).
   - Picture things happening the way you want.
   - Enroll the support of others.
   - Deal with obstacles positively.
6. Identify priorities and verbalize them (p. 178).
   - Know the difference between must-haves and nice-to-haves.
   - Rank order the nice-to-haves.

◆ Step F ◆ CUT YOUR LOSSES WHEN NECESSARY (pp. 178–182)

1. Keep a mental "tickler file" of the little things that don't fit (pp. 179–180).
   - When the words and the behavior don't match, believe the behavior.
   - Watch for the breaks in patterns.
   - Don't ignore the obvious.
2. Follow the Rule of Three (or Two) (pp. 180–181).
3. Have a system in place for cutting back your investment (p. 181).
   - Know how much money you will invest before you see a return.
   - Know how much time you will allow a problem to consume before you follow another course of action.
   - Know how much energy and ego you need to invest to "give it your best shot."

◆ Key IV ◆ | **PROVIDE FOR THE ROUTINE "CARE AND FEEDING" OF THE PROJECT TEAM (pp. 195–203)**

Rate your project using the seven main factors for project success (pp. 199–200).

Identify components of the coordination and relations factor that need work (pp. 200–201).

Give yourself a T-P balance check (pp. 201–203).

◆ Step A ◆ | **IDENTIFY THE INTERPERSONAL ROLES AND SKILLS NEEDED TO MAINTAIN AND COMPLETE GROUP ACTION (pp. 203–207)**

1. Recognize the roles and skills that direct energy to the task (p. 205). Be sure that someone will
   - initiate activity;
   - seek other opinions and information;
   - coordinate;
   - summarize.
2. Recognize the roles and skills that direct energy to the group (pp. 205–206). Be sure that someone will
   - follow;
   - gatekeep;
   - set standards;
   - express group feelings;
   - encourage.
3. Recognize the roles and skills that direct energy both to the task and to the group (p. 207).
   - Test for consensus.
   - Relieve tension.
   - Mediate.

◆ Step B ◆ | **ENCOURAGE GROUP PERFORMANCE OF THESE ROLES AND SKILLS (pp. 207–210)**

1. Pay attention (p. 208).
   - Don't ignore positive behavior from a difficult person.
   - Don't take for granted the positive behavior of a typically helpful person.

2. Give feedback (pp. 208–209) that is
   - specific;
   - measurable;
   - goal-related;
   - visual;
   - immediate.
3. Reinforce (pp. 209–210).
   - Use social reinforcers whenever possible.
   - Also use gadgets, signals, tokens, or consumables.

◆ Step C ◆ DEVELOP MISSING ROLES AND SKILLS IN OTHER TEAM MEMBERS WHEN POSSIBLE (pp. 210–212)

1. Delegate (p. 211).
2. Rotate assignments (p. 211).
3. Assign individual development activity (p. 211).
4. Lead or assign group development activity (p. 211).
5. Provide formal training (p. 211–212).

◆ Step D ◆ SUPPLY THE MISSING ROLES AND SKILLS WHEN NEEDED (p. 212)

1. Borrow a person to supply a role.
2. Hire an outside consultant to supply a role.
3. "Hire" a new person onto the team.
4. Supply the role yourself.

◆ Step E ◆ RECOGNIZE DYSFUNCTIONAL ROLES (pp. 220–233)

Recognize signs that your group is headed for Groupthink, Burnout, Demolition, or Collapse. See Table 13-1.

◆ Step F ◆ BALANCE THEM (pp. 220–233)

Supply antidotes. See Table 13-1.

Table 13–1
Signs of Misdirection and Antidotes

DIRECTION	GROUPTHINK Highly cohesive state of striving for consensus.	BURNOUT Isolation with depletion of physical and mental resources to attain a goal.	DEMOLITION The result of escalating infighting.	COLLAPSE Out of bounds project behavior.
DANGER	Bad technical decisions.	Project failure (from lack of team effort) or the sacrifice of individual team members.	"Explosion" of the team or the project or both.	Collapse of project from its own weight.
SYMPTOMS	Illusion of invulnerability Shared stereotypes Rationalization Illusion of morality Self censorship Mind guarding	Isolation Withdrawal Exhaustion	Blaming within Sarcasm Absence of response Temper explosions Gross overstatement Distortion of information Catastrophizing	False Starts "Efforting" Migrant objectives Out of bounds growth Abandonment
BENCHMARKS	Coffee Klatch Fraternity House	Isolation Withdrawal	Fighting Cubs Bumper Cars	False Starts "Efforting"
ANTIDOTES	Gatekeep. Seek other opinions and information. Follow. Test for consensus.	Gatekeep. Coordinate. Express group feeling. Encourage. Relieve tension.	Encourage. Relieve tension. Mediate. Set standards.	Gatekeep. Share information. Coordinate. Diagnose. Set standards. Mediate.

REFERENCES

Albrecht, Karl. *Stress and the Manager.* Englewood Cliffs, N.J.: Prentice-Hall, 1979, 29.

Allen, Thomas J. "Communication Networks in R & D Labs," *R & D Management, 1* (1970), 14–21.

Baker, Bruce, N.; Murphy, David C.; and Fisher, Dalmar. "Factors Affecting Project Management Success" in David I. Cleland and William R. King (Eds.) *Project Management Handbook.* New York: Van Nostrand Reinhold, 1983, 669–685.

Barnes, Donald W. "Linear Responsibility Charting," *Industrial Engineering,* July 1972, 17–19.

Bartolomé, Fernando and Evans, Paul A. Lee, "Must Success Cost So Much," *Harvard Business Review,* March-April 1980, 137–148.

Birnbaum, P. H.; Newell, W. T.; and Saxborg, B. O. "Managing Academic Interdisciplinary Research Projects," *Decision Sciences, 10* (4), October 1979, 645–665.

Blake, Robert R. and Mouton, Jane S. *The Managerial Grid.* Houston: Gulf Publishing Company, 1964.

Block, Peter. *Flawless Consulting.* Austin, Texas: Learning Concepts, 1981.

Brooks, John. *Telephone.* New York: Harper & Row, 1975.

Burrows, William E. "Cockpit Encounters," *Psychology Today,* November 1983, 43–47.

Carruth, E. "Genesco Comes to Judgment," *Fortune,* July 1975, 108–113, 178, 180.

Carruth, E. and others. "Genesco after the Judgment," *Fortune,* February 1977, 30, 32.

Clark, Thomas B. *Project Management and Control.* Atlanta: Young-Clark Associates, n. d.

Cummings, T. G.; Malloy, E. S.; and Glen, R. H. "Intervention Strategies for Improving Productivity and the Quality of Working Life," *Organizational Dynamics,* 1975, *4* (1), 52–68.

Dailey, R. C. "Project Leader's Locus of Control and Task Certainty as Antecedents of Members' Satisfaction and R & D Team Performance," *Engineering Management International, 1*(1), July 1981, 41–47.

Dailey, R. C. "Relationship between Locus of Control, Perceived Group Cohesiveness, and Satisfaction with Coworkers," *Psychological Reports*, 1978, *42*, 311–316.

Dalton, Gene W. and Thompson, Paul H. *Novations: Strategies for Career Management*. Glenview, Illinois: Scott, Foresman and Company, 1986.

Ehrbar, A. F. "Toil and Trouble at Continental Illinois," *Fortune*, February 7, 1983, 50–54, 56.

Freudenberger, Herbert J. *Burn-Out: The High Cost of High Achievement*. New York: Doubleday and Company, Inc., 1980.

Gibson, John E. *Managing Research and Development*. New York: John Wiley and Sons, 1981.

Gilbreath, Robert D. *Winning at Project Management*. New York: John Wiley and Sons, 1986.

Greiner, Larry E. and Schoin, Virginia E. "The Paradox of Managing a Project-Oriented Matrix: Establishing Coherence within Chaos," *Sloan Management Review, 22* (2), Winter 1981, 17–22.

Hill, R. E. "Managing interpersonal conflict in project teams," *Sloan Management Review, 18* (2), Winter 1977, 45–61.

Holt, Laurence. "Project Management Principles Succeed at ICI," *IMDS,* March–April 1983, 4–9.

House, Ruth S. Increase Training Benefits: Decrease Role Conflict, *Performance and Instruction, 21* (5), June 1982, 14–15.

Janis, Irving. *Group Dynamics: "Groupthink."* Del Mar, California: CRM McGraw-Hill Films, 1973 (Film).

Katz, R. "Effects of Group Longevity on Project Communication and Performance, *Administrative Science Quarterly, 27,* March 1982, 81–104.

Keister, Edwin, Jr. "The Playing Fields of the Mind," *Psychology Today,* July 1984, 18–24.

Kushner, Harold S. *When All You Ever Wanted Isn't Enough.* New York: Summit Books, 1986.

Lester, David. "Status Integration and Homicide," *Psychological Reports, 32* (3, Pt. 1), 1973, 774.

Linton, Calvin. *Effective Revenue Writing.* Washington, D.C.: U. S. Government Printing Office, 1962.

McFarlan, L. Warren. "Portfolio Approach to Information Systems," *Harvard Business Review, 59* (5), Sept.-Oct. 1981, 142–150.

Miles, Robert H. "Role Requirements as Sources of Organizational Stress." *Journal of Applied Psychology, 61* (2), 1976, 172–179.

Miles, Robert H. and Perrault, William D. "Organizational Role Conflict: Its Antecedents and Consequences." *Organizational Behavior and Human Performance,* 1976, 17 (1), 19–44.

Moolin, Frank P., Jr. "The 'managerial elite'—A Short Term Solution to the Effective Management of Giant Projects?" Paper presented to the James A. Henderson Memorial Lecture, Massachusetts Institute of Technology, Cambridge, MA: November 14, 1978.

Petroski, Henry. *To Engineer is Human.* New York: St. Martin's Press, 1986.

Pfeiffer, J. William and Jones, John E. (Eds.). *A Handbook of Structured Experiences for Human Relations Training,* Vol. I. La Jolla, California: University Associates, 1974, 7–12.

Redman, K. C. and Smith. T. M., "Lessons from Project Whirlwind." IEEE *Spectrum.* Vol. 14, No. 10, October 1977, 50–59.

Rice, Berkeley, "Can companies kill?" *Psychology Today, 115* (6), June 1981, 78, 79, 81, 82, 84, 85.

Rogers, Carl R. *On Becoming a Person.* Boston, MA: Houghton Mifflin Company, 1961.

Rotter, Julian B. "Generalized Expectancies for Internal versus External Control of Reinforcement." *Psychological Monographs, 80* (1), 1–28.

Schutz, William. *FIRO-B Scales Manual.* Palo Alto, CA: Consulting Psychologists Press, 1967. (Note: This reference available only with testing certification.)

Schutz, William. "The Interpersonal Underworld," *Harvard Business Review,* July–August 1958, 123–135.

Shull, Fremont A.; Delbecq, André L, and Cummings, L. L. *Organizational Decision Making.* New York: McGraw-Hill, 1970.

Slevin, Dennis P. "Leadership and the Project Manager" in David I. Cleland and William R. King (Eds.) *Project Management Handbook.* New York: Van Nostrand Reinhold, 1983, 567–580.

Smith, Hyrum W. *Focus on Time Management.* Salt Lake City, Utah: The Franklin Institute, 1986 (Audio tapes).

Thaimhain, H. J. and Wilemon, D. L. "Conflict Management in Project Life Cycles," *Sloan Management Review,* Spring, 1975, 31–50.

Winship, Barbara and Kelley, Jan. "A verbal response Model of Assertiveness," *Journal of Counseling Psychology, 23,* 215–220.

Woldeman, Albert W. *Lawyer Lincoln.* Boston: Houghton Mifflin Company, 1936, 172.

Index

Choosing The Right Management Tools

Locate the appropriate box for your project on the chart below. Then circle the management tools you expect to be most important to your project success.

- Formal control
- Formal planning
- External integration
- Internal integration

Table 4–3
Management Tools for Project Success

Experience with Technology	Outcomes	
	Loosely-defined Outcomes	Well-defined Outcomes
High Company Experience	Internal Integration External Integration	Internal Integration
Low Company Experience	External Integration Formal Control Formal Planning (if project is large)	Formal Control Formal Planning (if project is large)

Using External Integration

To provide external integration

1. Select clients as project team members. Look for the following:
   - Someone who is technically competent.
   - Someone who is an opinion leader.
   - Someone who has worked with you or with other team members before. (If this isn't possible, look for someone who has a good track record on interdepartmental projects.)

2. Place clients in key positions on project teams.
   - Assign specific roles for each meeting and rotate them: historian, conscience, gatekeeper, time keeper.
   - Let client know role assignment ahead of time.
   - Give client opportunity to represent the team publicly.

3. Involve clients in key decisions such as approval of specifications and key action dates.
   - Distribute agenda.
   - Distribute summary.

4. Clearly define areas of client responsibility.
   - Draft list of client responsibilities.
   - Revise for project agreement.
   - Establish change control procedure.

5. Communicate formally with other members of the client group.
   - Establish contact with key users.
   - Establish contact with every member of the client group who has a responsibility listed in the revised project agreement.

6. Communicate systematically with key people in the organization as a whole.
   - Keep in touch with the mainstream. Listen for answers to questions such as
     —Who are the decision makers and the gatekeepers?
     —What are people talking about? (What events, values, myths recur in conversation enough to be themes?)
     —Who speaks to whom? When? Why?

—What are the status symbols? Who's losing some? Who's gaining some?

—Where is the money going? Who's losing some? Who's gaining some?

—Where is the money coming from?

- When you talk to management

—ask for a commitment of time and attention;

—always be on time;

—always have a notebook and pen;

—always have an executive summary on the tip of your tongue;

—get to the point quickly;

—never allow a part of the truth to paint an inaccurate picture;

—never drop a bomb.

Providing Internal Integration

To provide internal integration:

1. Select experienced technical people to the project team.

2. Select team members who have worked together before. If that's not possible look for people with good track records on interdepartmental projects and
   - Be explicit about specific assignments;
   - Be explicit about group roles.

3. Select a compatible project manager (or *be* one!):
   - be there;
   - listen;
   - respond with respect.

4. Communicate within the team.
   - rotate roles;
   - distribute an agenda;
   - provide meeting summaries;
   - meet at the right intervals;
   - meet on the right day and at the right time;
   - meet at the right location;
   - seek consensus;
   - give support;
     —accept responsibility for problems;
     —give credit to team;
     —pass on compliments and add your own;
     —stay in touch;
   - be honest but not negative.

5. Involve team members in setting goals and deadlines:
   - provide agenda that includes action items and decisions you expect to surface;
   - provide summary including action items and decisions agreed upon.

6. Get outside technical assistance if
   - things are not going well at all;
   - things are going too well.

Visualizing People

Use the following chart to

1. list key people;
2. identify the technology of each key person;
3. rank order the technology by degree of abstractness;
4. place each key person on an organizational pyramid scaled to visualize the depth and the span of the project.

Analysis Chart: People and Pressures

1. **List Key People**	2. **Identify Technology**	3. **Rank** [0 = concrete x = very abstract]	
Official Decision Maker (DM)			
Opinion Leader (OL)			
Gatekeeper (G)			
Client (C)			
Team Member$_1$ (TM$_1$)			
Team Member$_2$ (TM$_2$)			
Team Member$_3$ (TM$_3$)			
Team Member$_4$ (TM$_4$)			
Team Member$_5$ (TM$_5$)			

4. Now place each key person on an organizational pyramid to visualize the depth and span of your project.

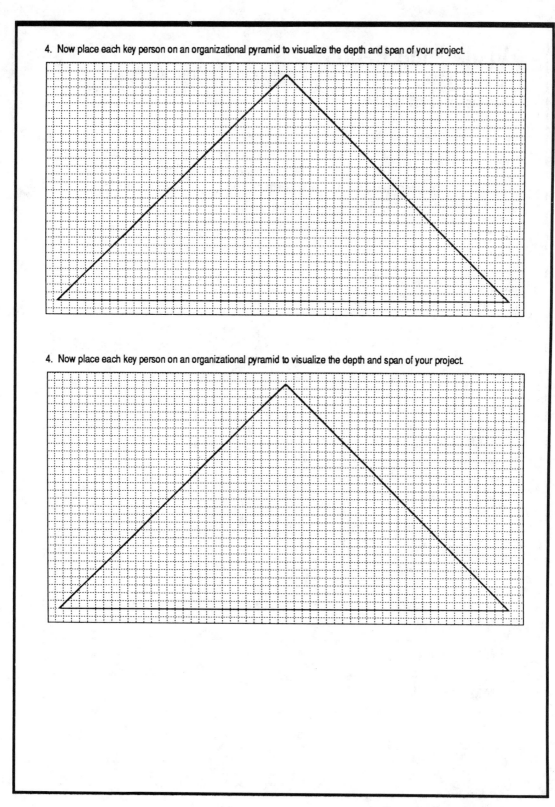

4. Now place each key person on an organizational pyramid to visualize the depth and span of your project.

Analyzing Pressures

Use the far right column of the same chart to note the impact of your project on each key individual.

Analysis Chart: People and Pressures

1. **List Key People**	2. **Identify Technology**	3. **Rank** [0 = concrete x = very abstract]	**Note Impact**
Official Decision Maker (DM)			
Opinion Leader (OL)			
Gatekeeper (G)			
Client (C)			
Team Member$_1$ (TM$_1$)			
Team Member$_2$ (TM$_2$)			
Team Member$_3$ (TM$_3$)			
Team Member$_4$ (TM$_4$)			
Team Member$_5$ (TM$_5$)			

Building a Negotiation Plan

Use the following worksheets to plan ways you can

1. collaborate in setting goals;
2. consult before a critical event to set parameters;
3. provide moral support;
4. secure the autonomy for each team member to do what needs to be done;
5. reinforce each person's effort to do what you want.

Notes for Negotiating

Collaborative Goal-Setting: _____

_____

_____

_____

Pre-event Consultation:

_____

_____

_____

_____

Support: _____

_____

_____

_____

_____

_____

Autonomy: _____

_____

_____

_____

Reinforcement: _____

_____

_____

_____

Notes for Negotiating

Collaborative Goal-Setting: _____

_____

_____

_____

Pre-event Consultation:

_____

_____

_____

_____

Support: _____

_____

_____

_____

_____

_____

Autonomy: _____

_____

_____

_____

Reinforcement: _____

_____

_____

_____

Notes for Negotiating

Collaborative Goal-Setting: _____

_____

_____

_____

Pre-event Consultation: _____

_____

_____

_____

_____

Support: _____

_____

_____

_____

_____

_____

Autonomy: _____

_____

_____

_____

Reinforcement: _____

_____

_____

_____

Notes for Negotiating

Collaborative Goal-Setting: _____

_____

_____

_____

Pre-event Consultation:

_____

_____

_____

_____

Support: _____

_____

_____

_____

_____

_____

Autonomy: _____

_____

_____

_____

Reinforcement: _____

_____

_____

_____

Organizing What You Know
About Key People

Use the following worksheets to record for each person, his or her

1. personal style;
2. relationship with you;
3. relationships with other key people;
4. pressures (job-related and other) to accept your ideas;
5. pressures (job-related and other) to resist your ideas.

Market Analysis of Key People

☐ The Official Decision-Maker: _____

☐ The Opinion Leader: _____

☐ The Gatekeeper: _____

☐ The Consumer: _____

Personal Style: _____

_____

_____

Relationship with You: _____

_____

_____

Relationships with Other Key People: _____

_____

_____

Pressure to Accept Idea

Job-Related	Other

Pressure to Resist Idea

Job-Related	Other

Market Analysis of Key People

☐ The Official Decision-Maker: _____

☐ The Opinion Leader: _____

☐ The Gatekeeper: _____

☐ The Consumer: _____

Personal Style: _____

_____

_____

Relationship with You: _____

_____

_____

Relationships with Other Key People: _____

_____

_____

Pressure to Accept Idea

Job-Related	Other

Pressure to Resist Idea

Job-Related	Other

Market Analysis of Key People

☐ The Official Decision-Maker: _____

☐ The Opinion Leader: _____

☐ The Gatekeeper: _____

☐ The Consumer: _____

Personal Style: _____

_____

_____

Relationship with You: _____

_____

_____

Relationships with Other Key People: _____

_____

_____

Pressure to Accept Idea

Job-Related	Other

Pressure to Resist Idea

Job-Related	Other

Market Analysis of Key People

☐ The Official Decision-Maker: _____

☐ The Opinion Leader: _____

☐ The Gatekeeper: _____

☐ The Consumer: _____

Personal Style: _____

_____

_____

Relationship with You: _____

_____

_____

Relationships with Other Key People: _____

_____

_____

Pressure to Accept Idea

Job-Related	Other

Pressure to Resist Idea

Job-Related	Other

Writing a Win-Win Script

Using the following worksheets:

1. incorporate a person's strongest job-related reason to resist your idea into an empathy statement (statement of the other person's point of view);
2. select a connecting word (like "but" or "however") to tell your listener you're changing directions;
3. incorporate a person's strongest job-related reason to accept your idea in a statement of the problem as you see it;
4. select a connecting word (like "so" or "therefore") to tell your listener there's more to come;
5. accommodate major nonjob related pressures in the course of action you recommend.

Script

Key Person _____

Empathy Statement

_____

_____

_____

_____

Connecting Word

_____

Statement of Problem as You See It

_____

_____

_____

_____

_____

Connecting Word

_____

Conclusion (request, call for action, decision)

_____

_____

_____

_____

_____

_____

_____

Script

Key Person _____

Empathy Statement

_____

_____

_____

_____

Connecting Word

_____

Statement of Problem as You See It

_____

_____

_____

_____

Connecting Word

_____

Conclusion (request, call for action, decision)

_____

_____

_____

_____

_____

_____

_____

Script

Key Person _____

Empathy Statement

_____

_____

_____

_____

Connecting Word

_____

Statement of Problem as You See It

_____

_____

_____

_____

_____

Connecting Word

_____

Conclusion (request, call for action, decision)

_____

_____

_____

_____

_____

_____

_____

Script

Key Person _____

Empathy Statement

_____

_____

_____

_____

Connecting Word

_____

Statement of Problem as You See It

_____

_____

_____

_____

_____

Connecting Word

_____

Conclusion (request, call for action, decision)

_____

_____

_____

_____

_____

_____

_____

Examining New Roles and Relationships

Ask yourself these questions about how the project manager's role will affect relationships.

1. How will relationships be affected by your new role to get work done through other people? What signals do you see that you are falling under Kepler's Law?
   - Are you pulling back decision-making authority that you have delegated?
     —Are you overinvolving yourself in work you have already delegated?
     —Are you focusing more and more intensely on procedures of greater and greater detail?
   - Does success seem more dependent on sheer endurance or brute strength than on skill or knowledge?

2. How will relationships be affected by your responsibility to develop team members?
   - Can you recognize development needs without feeling angry about them?
   - Will you take the time to develop your people instead of doing it all yourself?
   - Are you willing to let some people be better than others at some things, not as good as others at some things?

3. How will relationships be affected by your responsibility to set and track priorities?
   - Are you thinking about *whether* something should be done or just *how* it should be done?
   - Are you getting input about priorities from other team members? From your client? From management?
   - Are you following up without overcontrolling?

4. How will relationships be affected by your need to market your project?
   - Are you resisting this responsibility? (Do you feel you're being dragged into office politics against your will?)
   - Are you feeling angry toward people who aren't sold? Are you shutting them out?

5. How will relationships be affected by your need for routine contact with higher management and with your client?
   - Is it awkward for you to deal face-to-face with people at different levels?
   - Are you being overcritical?
   - Are you stifling your opinions?

Assessing Control In General

If possible, respond to the Rotter Scale. (Rotter, n. d., (1), 1–28.) If you did not complete this activity as you read the text of Chapter Seven, graph the highs and lows in your life on the chart below. Label them with life events.

Your Own Lifeline

AGE
0   5   10   15   20   25   30   35   40   45   50

Now go back and analyze the work related highs and lows. You can code them this way:

! I took a great risk.

* I played it safe.

0 Someone else made a major decision I thought should be mine.

+ I made one of my best decisions.

× I felt I had no control.

I was in control.

List the characteristics of the highs:

-
-
-
-
-

List the characteristics of the lows:

-
-
-
-
-

Studying Your Behavior

If possible, respond to the FIRO-B. (Available to certified professionals through Consulting Psychologists Press, Palo Alto, CA.)

Answer these questions about your relationships with other key people.

1. Around which people do you feel crowded? These people may want to include you more than you want to be included.

   _____

   _____

2. Around which people do you feel left out? You may want to be included more than these people want to include you.

   _____

   _____

3. Around which people do you feel pushed? These people may want to control you more than you want them to.

   _____

   _____

4. Around which people do you feel directionless? You may want these people to exert more control than they want.

   _____

   _____

5. Around which people do you feel smothered? These people may want to give you more affection than you want to receive.

   _____

   _____

6. Around which people do you feel rejected? These people may give you less affection than you want.

_____

_____

Choosing the Best Course of Action

Your answers to these questions can help you choose.

1. Does the difference between what you want and what you're getting matter? _____. If it doesn't, just live and let live.

2. Is it clear that your own behavior is out of line? _____.
   Is the cost of changing your behavior small while the cost to the other person of changing his behavior is great? _____.
   Is the other person unable to change? _____.

   If the answer to these questions is yes, consider modifying your own behavior.

3. Is it clear that something about a relationship is getting in the way but not clear what to do about it? _____.
   If you answered yes then give and get feedback about how behavior preferences are affecting the relationship or the project.

4. Does the behavior matter? _____. Would a change in your behavior alone harm the project? _____. Is at least part of the solution clear? _____.

   If you answered yes to all three questions then negotiate for a change in the other person's behavior.

Planning to Handle Conflict

Use the following chart to identify those sources of conflict most likely to be intense during the current phase of your project.

Survey Rankings of Seven Sources of Conflict

	Project Formulation	Build-Up	Main Program	Phase-Out
Schedules	3	2	1	1
Priorities	1	1	4	4
Manpower	4	5	3	3
Technical Issues	6	4	2	6
Administration	2	3	5	7
Personality	7	6	7	2
Cost	5	7	6	5

1. Find the rankings for the current phase of your project.

2. Rank the sources of conflict as you see them.

3. How do your rankings compare with those in the survey?

Top Three Sources
in Survey

Top Three Sources
in Your Ranking

1. _____

1. _____

2. _____

2. _____

3. _____

3. _____

4. If your rankings vary drastically from those in the survey, get a second opinion. Ask a team member or a confidante who has knowledge of the project to rank the sources. How do his rankings compare with your own?

What conflicts in your project up to this point do you suspect of being personality conflicts in disguise?

_____

_____

_____

_____

Which has been your preferred style of dealing with conflict in previous projects (or up to this point in the current project)?

_____ Withdrawal   _____ Forcing

_____ Smoothing   _____ Confrontation

_____ Compromising

Which style will you try to rely on more for the rest of this project? _____

Which style will you rely on less? _____

Use the following chart to find the most likely focus of persistent conflict on

your project. What is the most likely focus? _____

_____

Table 8–7
Attributes of a Project and Focus of Conflict

	Extent of Agreement on Outcomes	
Experience with Technology	Loosely-defined Outcomes	Well-defined Outcomes
High Company Experience	Conflict within Team and Conflict between Team and the Outside Equally High	Higher Conflict within Team
Low Company Experience	Higher Conflict between Team and the Outside	Both Equally Low

Which questions about individual roles are generating conflict for key people in your project?

- Who is asking "Am I in or out?" "Do I belong in this group or not?"

_____

_____

_____

- Who is asking "Am I top or bottom?" "How will the group make decisions?" "How much responsibility, how much influence, how much control will I have?"

_____

_____

_____

- Who is asking "Am I near or far?" "How close should I get?" "How much of myself should I share?" "How much should I care?" "How much could I be hurt?"

_____

_____

_____

Use the following "market analysis" to analyze someone who is stuck on one of those questions about individual roles. Then, use the next worksheet to script an approach to that person.

Market Analysis of Someone Who Is Stuck

☐ The Official Decision-Maker: _____

☐ The Opinion Leader: _____

☐ The Gatekeeper: _____

☐ The Consumer: _____

Personal Style: _____

_____

_____

Relationship with You: _____

_____

_____

Relationships with Other Key People: _____

_____

_____

Pressure to Accept Idea

Job-Related	Other

Pressure to Resist Idea

Job-Related	Other

Script to Use with Someone Who Is Stuck

Key Person _____

Empathy Statement

_____

_____

_____

_____

Connecting Word

_____

Statement of Problem as You See It

_____

_____

_____

_____

_____

Connecting Word

_____

Conclusion (request, call for action, decision)

_____

_____

_____

_____

_____

_____

_____

_____

Managing Stress

1. Answer these questions to help you recognize a stressful situation in time to do something about it.

   • Identify some past situations in which your stress load has gone beyond your personal Plimsoll line:

   _____

   _____

   _____

   _____

   _____

   _____

   • What signals did you get from your body when you passed (or were approaching) the Plimsoll line?

   _____   _____

   _____   _____

   _____   _____

   • Which of these signals is your body giving you now?

   _____   _____

   _____   _____

   _____   _____

2. Answer these questions to find ways to tell yourself you can handle the situation calmly.

- How can you reply to the negative voices in your head? Write out a response to one of the voices. If the voices are predicting catastrophe (with words like "ruined," "devastated," "disastrous"), you predict control (with phrases like "embarrassed, but . . ," "disappointed, but . . ," "difficult, but. . . ."). Replace each catastrophic word with something that is both more realistic and more manageable.

_____

_____

_____

_____

_____

- What humor do you find in the situation? Would some of this be funny if it were happening to someone else? (Then try to laugh at yourself.) Can you imagine this situation from a scene in a farce? (Keystone Cops? Young Frankenstein?) If you designed a T-shirt for your team, what slogan would be written on it?

- How can you work smarter instead of harder?

  Do you spend at least twenty minutes planning each day?
  Do you get unpleasant tasks out of the way first?
  Do you let go of delegated tasks?
  Do you say "No" when you should?

- Have you cleared space in your day for relaxation and exercise?

- Do you assert yourself without being insensitive to others?

Being a "Lightning Rod"

Briefly describe a project conflict during which your effort to deal with the situation calmly was met with a direct attack.

_____

_____

_____

_____

_____

How did you respond to the attack? If you remember your exact behavior and your exact words, write them out.

_____

_____

_____

_____

_____

Rate your response on how well it compares with the characteristics of managers of successful projects (Hill, 1977, pp. 45–61). If your response fully demonstrated a characteristic, give yourself a 5 for that characteristic. If your response totally omitted a characteristic, give yourself a 0 for that characteristic.

____ Personally absorbed aggression (served as a "lightning rod")
____ Set an example of listening
____ Counseled
____ Encouraged openness and emotional expression
____ Served as a role model
____ Paced and controlled potential conflict when possible
____ Sensed some usefulness in the conflict

Now visualize that situation happening again. Mentally rehearse the way you would do the following:

1. Put yourself on hold.
   - Picture yourself remaining quiet, even if your instinctive reaction is to lash out.
   - See your mind as a blank screen with your thoughts, your feelings erased.

2. Screen out distractions.
   - Picture yourself facing the other person in the conflict, sitting about three feet apart on the same side of the desk.
   - Picture yourself leaning toward the other person at a 20° or 30° angle with your feet flat on the ground.
   - Picture yourself making direct eye contact with a relaxed expression on your face.

3. Give it some time. Picture yourself remaining quiet and relaxed for 10 seconds after the other person has finished speaking.

4. Respond to both the feeling content and the factual content of the situation. Complete the blanks in this statement. Then picture (and hear) yourself saying it to the other person in the conflict.

"Sounds like you feel _____ because _____

_____ ."

Excavating the Issue

1. Identify three ways you could treat the issue as it was originally presented as real.

_____

_____

_____

_____

_____

_____

_____

2. Fill in the following Assertive Script to show how you would begin to excavate if the conflict persists.

3. Fill in a Linear Responsibility Chart for your project so far. (You may want to make this a team project.)

What features of your chart surprise you? _____

_____

_____

_____

What else did you learn from it?

_____

_____

_____

_____

4. List three to five specific ways you can give another person in the project support without agreeing with him.

_____

_____

_____

_____

_____

_____

_____

_____

_____

_____

_____

Assertive Script

Key Person _____

Empathy Statement

_____

_____

_____

_____

Connecting Word

_____

Statement of Problem as You See It

_____

_____

_____

_____

Connecting Word

_____

Conclusion (request, call for action, decision)

_____

_____

_____

_____

_____

_____

_____

Table 9–3
Blank Linear Responsibility Chart

RESPONSIBILITIES
A. Authorizes
B. Coordinates outside division
C. Supervises
D. Completes
E. Must be consulted
F. Must approve final product/service

Project Life Cycle
Formulation Phase.

1. Identify need.
2. Develop an initial response plan.
3. Test feasibility of initial response.
4. Generate alternate strategies to meet response objectives.
5. Answer these questions to set parameters:
   What will the response cost?
   When will it be ready?
   What will it do?
   How will it fit into existing systems?
6. Design tentative project system.
7. Define relationships (interfaces).
8. Identify human and technical resources needed.
9. Assign project manager.

Buildup Phase.

1. Develop project organization.

Key People

Management
- Bedford Haynes, President
- Edward Dalton, Sr. V.P.
- Walter Pruitt, Engineering Mgr.

Project Team
- Carl White, Engineering
- Brad Thornton, Production
- Enid Schwartz, Methods & Standards
- Jack Thompson, Quality Assurance
- Fred Kemp, Maintenance

Support Staff
- (Not yet assigned)

Users
- Edward Dalton [See Mgt. Col.]
- Mark Johnson, Production
- Chris Latham, Methods & Standards
- Walter Pruitt [See Mgt. Col.]
- Helen Kraus, Quality Assurance
- Jeff Moore, Maintenance

2. Define final system performance requirements.

3. Develop detailed project plans.

4. Define in detail relationships needed within the project.

5. Define in detail relationships needed between the project system and the outside. (Include transfer of responsibility to user and the reassignment of staff.)

6. Identify support needed.

7. Develop policies and procedures.

8. Complete staffing.

Main Program Phase.

1. Update detailed project plans.

2. Verify performance standards.

3. Develop, produce, and install product or service.

4. Test.

5. Feedback results and act on them.

6. Identify support needed during operation.

7. Develop users' manual.

8. Monitor operation by user.

9. Integrate product or service into user's system.

10. Evaluate operation.

Phase-Out.

1. Refine plans to transfer responsibility from project team to user.

2. Transfer responsibility.

3. Establish followup system.

4. Explore and report lessons learned.

5. Reassign staff

Looking at Your Response to Conflict

Briefly describe a conflict situation in which you felt under attack. (You may want to review the situation you described under "Being a Lightning Rod.")

_____

_____

_____

_____

Now circle the paragraphs in the following chart that describe your response.

Physical Conflict vs. Emotional Conflict

Success Strategy for Physical Conflict	Success Strategy for Emotional Conflict
Adrenalin: The surge of adrenalin ("Fight or Flight") is functional.	**Adrenalin:** The "Fight or Flight" response is nonfunctional—even damaging. It can increase blood pressure and pulse rate, for example, with no outlet.
Best Peace Strategy: To show strength • Stay on guard. • Leave no vulnerable position.	**Best Peace Strategy:** To show strength • Let down guard. • Show confidence by being open to vulnerability.
Physical Stance: Square _off_ to display strength and intimidate opponent.	**Physical Stance:** Square _away_ to establish equality and invite the other person.
Mental Stance: • Size up the opponent. • Evaluate the opponent's strengths and weaknesses.	**Mental Stance:** Reflect nonjudgmentally.
Most Valuable Data: Pay attention to verifiable fact.	**Most Valuable Data:** Pay attention to "fuzzies."
Control: To limit the conflict use • Containment. • "Divide and conquer" strategy.	**Control:** Limit conflict through • Opening up. • Exposing vulnerability.
Speed: • Be swift. • Be sure.	**Speed:** • Pace the conflict. • Individualize the response.

How many paragraphs did you circle under physical conflict? _____

How many did you circle under emotional conflict? _____

Describe three things you would do differently if you were to relive this situation:

_____

_____

_____

_____

_____

Looking for Win-Win Alternatives

1. Write out the outcomes you are hoping for in this conflict. Are you trying to teach ducks to sing? Go back and rate the outcomes as doable or undoable.

Doable	Undoable	Outcomes
Check One		

2. If you have done an earlier market analysis of this situation, review it now. If you have not, do a market analysis here using the worksheet on the next page.

Market Analysis Worksheet

☐ The Official Decision-Maker: _____

☐ The Opinion Leader: _____

☐ The Gatekeeper: _____

☐ The Consumer: _____

Personal Style: _____

_____

_____

Relationship with You: _____

_____

_____

Relationships with Other Key People: _____

_____

_____

Pressure to Accept Idea

Job-Related	Other

Pressure to Resist Idea

Job-Related	Other

3. If you have developed an earlier assertive statement for this situation, review it now. If you have not, write an assertive script here using the following worksheet. Remember

- Use the strongest job-related pressure to resist in your statement of the other person's point of view.
- Incorporate the strongest job-related reason to support in the statement of the problem as you see it.
- Accommodate as many nonjob-related pressures as you can in the course of action you propose.

Assertive Script Worksheet

Key Person _____

Empathy Statement

_____

_____

_____

_____

Connecting Word

_____

Statement of Problem as You See It

_____

_____

_____

_____

_____

Connecting Word

_____

Conclusion (request, call for action, decision)

_____

_____

_____

_____

_____

_____

_____

_____

Look at things right side up

Begin by answering these questions to separate the people and the situation:

What *is* happening that you wish *were not* happening?

_____

_____

_____

_____

_____

_____

What *is not* happening that you wish *were* happening?

_____

_____

_____

_____

What would need to happen in order for you to say "This situation is no longer a problem"?

_____

_____

_____

_____

Now separate *what* needs to be done from *how* it might get done.

Describe the "how's" you have locked into that might keep you from reaching the "what."

_____

_____

_____

_____

_____

_____

Next distinguish between your emotions and reality. Rewrite some of the catastrophic things you think or say about the situation to realistically depict the situation as more manageable.

Catastrophic Statement   Realistic Description

_____   _____

_____   _____

_____   _____

_____   _____

_____   _____

_____   _____

Picture the situation turning out well

Describe the details you see that confirm things are going right—what you feel, what you see, what you taste, what you hear, what you smell.

_____

_____

_____

_____

_____

_____

Identify your priorities and verbalize them

List the absolute must-haves here.

_____

_____

_____

_____

_____

List the "nice-to-haves" here. Rank them from one (would add the most value) to X (would add the least value).

_____

_____

_____

_____

_____

_____

Cutting Your Losses

What little things haven't fit?

List the inconsistencies that could be signs of resistance or alienation.

_____ _____

_____ _____

_____ _____

_____ _____

_____ _____

_____ _____

Follow the Rule of Two (or Three)

Write out your statement to confront an inconsistency the second or third time that it occurs.

_____

_____

_____

_____

When and how can you withdraw your investment if the losses become too great?
- How much money will you invest before you see a return? _____
  What will you do to halt your investment?

_____

_____

_____

_____

- How much time will you allow the problem to consume before you take another course of action? _____

- What other course of action will you take?

  _____

  _____

  _____

  _____

- How will you limit preoccupation with the losses at work?

  _____

  _____

  _____

  _____

- How will you limit spillover of the problem into your personal life?

  _____

  _____

  _____

  _____

Reviewing Team Effort

On the following chart, check the adjectives you think describe the way key people feel about your project.

	Very Satisfied	Satisfied	Dissatisfied
Key people in the parent organization	_____	_____	_____
Key people on the project team	_____	_____	_____
Key people in the client organization as a whole	_____	_____	_____
Key users within the client organization	_____	_____	_____

Now rate your project on the aspects of coordination and relations (1 = we're doing very well, 5 = we're doing very poorly):

_____ project team spirit

_____ project team participation in decision making

_____ project team sense of mission

_____ project team participation in major problem solving

_____ project team goal commitment

_____ supportive internal team relations

_____ project team capability

_____ project manager's human skills

_____ project manager's administrative skills

_____ project manager's authority

_____ unity between project manager and contributing department managers

_____ unity between project manager and his own manager

_____ job security of the project team

_____ enthusiasm of parent organization

_____ unity between project manager and public officials

_____ unity between project manager and client contact

_____ realistic progress reports

_____ availability of backup strategies

Now check every characteristic of a gatekeeper you feel applies to you.

_____ I consult significantly more often with organizational colleagues.

_____ I spend significantly more time in these consultations.

_____ I rely on more people both within my own specialty and outside their specialty.

_____ I show the only real contact outside my own specialty.

_____ I read more—especially more hard literature.

_____ I maintain relationships outside my organization that are broader ranging and longer lasting.

Identifying Needed Roles

Put a check by the roles you feel are already well-supplied in your team. Circle the ones that still need to be supplied.

1. Roles that direct energy to the task
   —Seek other opinions and information
   —Initiate activity
   —Coordinate
   —Summarize

2. Roles that direct energy to the group
   —Follow
   —Gatekeep
   —Set standards
   —Express group feeling
   —Encourage

3. Roles that direct energy toward the task and toward the group
   —Test for consensus
   —Relieve tension
   —Mediate

Encouraging Performance

What team members are supplying the roles you checked above? How will you reinforce their behavior (social reinforcers, gadgets, signals, tokens, consumables)?

Role	Supplier	Reinforcement You Can Provide

Developing Missing Roles

Which roles that you circled can you develop in team members (delegate, assign individual development activity, lead or assign group development activity, rotate assignments, provide formal training)?

Role	Supplier	How You Will Develop Role

Supplying Missing Roles

Which roles circled must you supply in some other way? How will you do it (borrow a person, hire an outside consultant, hire a new person on to the team, supply the role yourself)?

Role   How You Will Supply It

_____   _____

                  _____

_____   _____

                  _____

_____   _____

                  _____

Recognizing and Balancing Dysfunctional Roles

On the following chart, circle the early symptoms of potential failure you have seen in your project.

Symptoms of Failure and Their Antidotes

DIRECTION	GROUPTHINK Highly cohesive state of striving for consensus.	BURNOUT Isolation with depletion of physical and mental resources to attain a goal.	DEMOLITION The result of escalating infighting.	COLLAPSE Out of bounds project behavior.
SYMPTOMS	Illusion of Invulnerability Shared stereotypes Rationalization Illusion of morality Self censorship Mind guarding	Isolation Withdrawal Exhaustion	Blaming within Sarcasm Absence of response Temper explosions Gross overstatement Distortion of information Catastrophizing	False Starts "Efforting" Migrant objectives Out of bounds growth Abandonment
ANTIDOTES	Gatekeep. Seek other opinions and information. Follow. Test for consensus.	Gatekeep. Coordinate. Express group feeling. Encourage. Relieve tension.	Encourage. Relieve tension. Mediate. Set standards.	Gatekeep. Share information. Coordinate. Diagnose. Set standards. Mediate.

Next, use the same chart to identify those roles you can use to get your project back on target.

Now, note specific actions you will take to activate the roles you identified.

Gatekeep. _____

_____

_____

_____

Seek other opinions and information. _____

_____

_____

_____

Follow. _____

_____

_____

_____

Test for consensus. _____

_____

_____

_____

Coordinate. _____

_____

_____

_____

Express group feeling. _____

_____

_____

_____

Encourage. _____

_____

_____

_____

Relieve tension. _____

_____

_____

_____

Mediate. _____

_____

_____

_____

Set standards. _____

_____

_____

_____

Share information. _____

_____

_____

_____

Diagnose. _____

_____

_____

_____